Withdrawn

OPTIMISM
PRESS

HOW TO
MAKE A PLANT
LOVE YOU

HOW TO MAKE A PLANT LOVE YOU

Cultivate Green Space in Your
Home and Heart

. . . .

SUMMER RAYNE OAKES

ILLUSTRATIONS BY MARK CONLAN

OPTIMISM PRESS

OPTIMISM PRESS
An imprint of Penguin Random House LLC
penguinrandomhouse.com

Most Optimism Press books are available at a discount when purchased in quantity for
sales promotions or corporate use. Special editions, which include personalized covers,
excerpts, and corporate imprints, can be created when purchased in large quantities. For more
information, please call (212) 572-2232 or email specialmarkets@penguinrandomhouse.com.
Your local bookstore can also assist with discounted bulk purchases using the Penguin
Random House corporate Business-to-Business program. For assistance in locating
a participating retailer, email B2B@penguinrandomhouse.com.

Library of Congress Cataloging-in-Publication Data

Names: Oakes, Summer Rayne, author.
Title: How to make a plant love you : cultivate green space in your home and heart /
Summer Rayne Oakes ; illustrations by Mark Conlan.
Description: New York City : Optimism Press, [2019] |
Includes bibliographical references and index.
Identifiers: LCCN 2019010935 (print) | LCCN 2019015413 (ebook) |
ISBN 9780525540298 (ebook) | ISBN 9780525540281 (hardcover)
Subjects: LCSH: House plants. | Gardening—Health aspects. |
Gardening—Psychological aspects.
Classification: LCC SB419 (ebook) | LCC SB419 .O25 2019 (print) | DDC 635.9/65—dc23
LC record available at https://lccn.loc.gov/2019010935

Printed in the United States of America
1 3 5 7 9 10 8 6 4 2

BOOK DESIGN BY LUCIA BERNARD

Penguin is committed to publishing works of quality and integrity.
In that spirit, we are proud to offer this book to our readers; however,
the story, the experiences, and the words are the author's alone.

To the plants: my teachers, my partners, and my compatriots,
for I have learned so much from you over the years.

and

To all the Crazy Plant People out there who have
ever fallen in love with a plant.

May you go forth and sow your homes and the earth with green.

CONTENTS

A LETTER FROM SIMON SINEK

The vision is clear: to build a world in which the vast majority of people wake up every single morning inspired, feel safe at work, and return home fulfilled at the end of the day. I believe the best way to build the world I imagine is with leaders. Good leaders. Great leaders. And so, I've devoted my professional life to finding, building, and supporting the leaders who are committed to leading in a way that will more likely bring that vision to life.

Unfortunately, the practice of leadership is so misunderstood. It has nothing to do with rank. It has nothing to do with authority. Those things may come with a leadership position—and they may help a leader operate with greater efficiency and at greater scale—but those things do not a leader make. Leadership is not about being in charge; it's about taking care of those in our charge. It is a distinctly human endeavor. And part of what it takes to advance good leadership is to share the lessons, tools, and ideas that help each of us become the leaders we wish we had. *How to Make a Plant Love You* is one of those ideas.

I fell in love with this concept because, at its core, *How to Make a Plant Love You* is a metaphor for how we view, and often treat, people. It is a direct but gentle reminder to consider how much the environment around us matters. Think about how we usually treat the plants in our homes: we find one we like, we place it in a room where we want it to go, where we think it looks best, and then we expect it to thrive. That strategy, unfortunately, only increases the chances that the plant will struggle or die. We first have to understand the plant in order to create the conditions for it to thrive—the same is true for people.

Too often, we find someone whose experience fits a job we need done. We put them in that job, in a space, and expect them to thrive. Unfortunately, such a strategy also increases the likelihood that someone will struggle to do well, or fail to work to their natural best. But there is a solution.

For some, *How to Make a Plant Love You* is a book about how we care for and treat our plants. However, if we embrace the underlying philosophies, we will find valuable life lessons that will teach us how to better care for and treat *people*—starting with ourselves. Summer Rayne takes us on a journey to show us how the environment we set significantly impacts the life and lives around us. If we can learn to ask what a plant needs from us, and not what we need from a plant, we will also learn how to ask that same question of people. This shift in mind-set is what servant leadership is all about. And if we can all learn to make that shift, it's amazing how alive our spaces, our communities, and our lives can be.

Happy planting and inspire on!

Simon Sinek

FOREWORD BY WADE DAVIS

This book is a love story that invites everyone to embrace the wonder of the botanical realm—all the glorious species of orchids and begonias, aroids and fuchsias, the delicate ferns and otherworldly bromeliads that flourish in the wild and can so readily be brought into our homes and lives. In sharing how plants transformed her life, Summer Rayne Oakes offers a practical guide that will allow you to discover, as she did, a relationship that is both rewarding and revelatory.

As Summer Rayne shares her delightful journey—one that led a peripatetic eco-activist and global fashion model to become a home-based, plant-inspired, urban apartment–dwelling horticultural guru—she confronts us with a fundamental paradox: we all love nature. Plants account for 80 percent of the world's biomass, yet most of us know almost nothing about botany. We may be familiar with hundreds of commercial brands, yet incapable of naming a single species of flowering plant.

Plants are the foundation of all sentient existence. The miracle of photosynthesis allows green leaves to harness the energy of the sun, producing food and releasing oxygen into the atmosphere, without which none of us could live. Children in all nations are encouraged to recite patriotic slogans, lines of verse, prayers, and popular ditties, yet not one in a million is asked to commit to the fundamental formula of life: the metabolic pathway by which carbon dioxide and water, sparked by photons of light, is transformed into carbohydrates and oxygen.

I say this not in judgement, for I too was raised blithely unaware of the deep significance of plants. Like Summer Rayne, I grew up with a keen appreciation of nature, and spent all of my waking hours exploring the forests and mountains of home. And though I would eventually earn a PhD in biology with a specialty in ethnobotany, I never took a course in botany until my third year of university. In my youth, and certainly through high school, I associated academic biology with formaldehyde, pickled rats, and white-frocked technicians in laboratory classrooms that smelled of chemicals. Only in time would I discover that while some biology teachers may indeed be boring, plants never are, and the study of botany is actually a window that opens wide to reveal the sacred essence of life itself.

At twenty, I first experienced the overwhelming grandeur of the Amazon rain forest. It is a subtle thing. There are few flowers to be seen, and certainly no cascades of orchids—just a thousand shades of green; an infinitude of shape, form, and texture. To sit in silence is to hear the constant hum of biological activity—evolution, if you will, working in overdrive. From the edge of trails creepers lash at the base of trees, and herbaceous heliconias and calatheas give way to broad-leaf aroids that climb into the shadows. Overhead, lianas drape from immense trees binding the canopy of the forest into a single interwoven fabric of life.

At first, knowing little of plants, I experienced the tropical forest only as a tangle of forms, shapes, and colors without meaning or depth; beautiful when taken as a whole but ultimately incomprehensible and exotic. But once viewed through the botanical lens, the components of the mosaic suddenly had names, the names implied relationships, and the relationships resonated with significance. This, for me, was the great revelation of botany.

My partner on this journey of discovery was the late Timothy Plowman, the protégé of the legendary Amazonian plant explorer, Richard Evans Schultes. In the mid-1970s, on a journey inspired by our great professor (made possible by his generosity and infused at all times with his spirit), Tim and I traveled the length of South America, traversing the Andes to reach the cloud forests and remote drainages that fell away into the Amazon. Tim was an inspired mentor, a dear friend, and a brilliant botanist—one of the very few capable of realigning taxonomic classifications simply by holding a blossom to the light.

Even as Tim and I worked our way south, collecting several thousand herbarium specimens along with great quantities of live material destined for the botanical gardens of the world, a book appeared that made a great fuss about houseplants responding to music and human voices. Tim found the entire notion slightly ridiculous. "Why would a plant give a shit about Mozart?" he asked. "And even if it did, why should *that* impress us? I mean, they can eat light. Isn't that enough?"

Tim went on to speak of photosynthesis the way an artist might describe color. He said that at dusk the process is reversed and plants actually emit small amounts of light. He referred to sap as the green blood of plants, explaining that chlorophyll is structurally almost the same as the pigment of our blood, only the iron in hemoglobin is replaced by magnesium in plants. He spoke of the way plants grow: a seed of grass producing sixty miles (96.6 kilometers) of root hairs in a day, 6,000 miles (9,656 kilometers) over the course of a season; a field of hay exhaling 500 tons of water into the air each day; a flower pushing its blossom through three inches of pavement; a single catkin of a birch tree producing 5 million grains of pollen; a tree living for 4,000 years. The trunk of a western hemlock, a miracle of biological engineering, stores thousands of gallons of water and supports branches festooned with as many as 70 million needles, all capturing the light of the sun. Spread out on the ground, the needles of a single tree would create a photosynthetic surface ten times the size of a football field.

Unlike every other botanist I had known, Tim was not obsessed with classification. For him Latin names were like koans or lines of verse. He remembered them effortlessly, taking particular delight in their origins. "When you say the names of the plants," he told me, "you say the names of the gods."

Among our many botanical discoveries during those long months of fieldwork were a number of new hallucinogens, uncovered through an ongoing series of self-experiments. Professor Schultes once quipped that Tim and I ate our way through the forests and hedgerows of the Andes and upper Amazon. In the wake of one of these curious sessions, I was inspired to share a revelation with our beloved yet famously conservative professor. On a bit of cardboard found discarded in the desert, I sketched a simple line that I intended to later dispatch to Harvard by telegram. "Dear Professor Schultes," the note read. "We are all ambulatory plants." Tim urged caution, and mercifully the message was never sent.

Inauspicious as such a missive may have been in the moment, it nevertheless conveyed essential truths. Life emerged from the sea. Animals went walking. Plants rooted themselves to place. Animals developed organs that concentrated all the functions essential to survival. Plants, by contrast, dispersed these functions throughout the entire organism, employing the entire body to breathe and create food through the processes of respiration and photosynthesis. Plants did not evolve brains because such a decentralized structure of production did not require one. Every green surface generates food. The wonder of plants, as Tim would say, is not the possibility that they respond to Mozart, Beethoven, or the Beatles, but rather in how they actually exist. To suggest that they communicate with the human sphere on our terms is a conceit that reveals, as much as anything, a failure to appreciate what plants as living organisms have actually achieved over millions of years of intense evolutionary pressure and competition.

This should not suggest for a moment that science has revealed all there is to know about the botanical realm. As Summer Rayne writes in this marvelous book, plants continue to amaze, displaying capacities difficult to explain, capabilities that defy the limits of our imaginings. Take, for example, the common *Mimosa pudica*, a ground cover known to many as the sensitive plant. Touch the leaves and they fold defensively, only slowly regaining their normal display with photosynthetic surfaces fully exposed to the sun. But do this several times to the same plant and it will, at some point, no longer respond to tactile stimuli. One can only conclude that in some idiosyncratic plant way, it no longer senses danger in your touch. And this surely suggests some kind of capacity for memory, at least of a kind.

Yet another sign of deliberate intent on the part of plants may be found in the temperate rain forests of the Pacific Northwest. The foundation of these forests are the mycelia of hundreds of species of fungi. Mycelia are the vegetative phase of a fungus, small hair-like filaments that spread through the organic layer at the surface of the soil, absorbing food and precipitating decay. A mushroom is simply the fruiting structure, the reproductive body. As the mycelia grow, they constantly encounter tree roots. If the species combination is the right one, a remarkable biological event unfolds. Fungus and tree come together to form mycorrhizae, a symbiotic partnership that allows both to benefit. The tree provides the fungus with sugars created from sunlight. The mycelia in turn enhance the tree's ability to absorb nutrients and water from the soil. They also produce growth-regulating chemicals that promote the production of new roots and enhance the immune system. Without this union, no tree could thrive. Western hemlocks are so dependent on mycorrhizal fungi that their roots barely pierce the surface of the earth, even as their trunks soar into the canopy. And the story only gets better. Researchers over the last years have discovered that individual trees selectively disperse sugars through the mycelia network, ensuring that top priority goes to seedlings of the mother tree, followed in decreasing order to seedlings of the same species, and finally to other botanical denizens of the forest. The tree knows its own, as surely as a mother can sense the presence of her own child.

Plants can also see, or so it seems in at least one instance of botanical adaptation. *Boquila trifoliolata* is a monotypic genus of flowering plants in the family Lardizabalaceae, native to the temperate forests of central and southern Chile and Argentina. The climbing vine produces a flush of leaves that mimic the shape, size, and form of the foliage of the host tree. But should, by chance, its tendrils reach for the support of a second and distinct species, the same individual boquila vine will sprout leaves echoing the appearance of the second host. To be capable of such a sleight of hand the vine must surely have some sense of what its neighbors look like, and it does: exterior cells act as a crude lens bringing into focus the morphology of both host plants.

All of this is to say that we need not invoke the mystic—or, in our hubris, imbue plants with human attributes—in order to appreciate their wonder. As Summer Rayne writes in this playful yet inspired guidebook, one need only plant a seed to watch the full miracle of botanical life unfold.

A NOTE BEFORE WE BEGIN

This book is intended as a relationship guide of sorts—a handbook for bringing plants and plant knowledge into your world, discovering their wonderful ways, and letting this special relationship add new dimensions to your life. While it isn't a technical treatise, there are terms, like plant names and parts, that may be unfamiliar but that are helpful to know when exploring plants and how they, and we, can flourish together. When possible, I'll elaborate on these terms, providing definitions or metaphors, in order to help you grasp these perhaps-foreign concepts.

When I first mention a plant species, I'll refer to it by its botanical Latin (scientific) name, which is a way to group, categorize, and identify plants more easily. This is to reduce confusion, as common and vernacular names for plants vary widely. For example, *Monstera deliciosa*, which has very large, fenestrated (some would say "monstrous") leaves and delicious, edible fruits (hence the epithet, *deliciosa*), has common names that include Mexican breadfruit, Swiss cheese plant, and fruit salad plant. I may use a plant's common name, but only after first introducing the plant by its botanical or scientific name.

But even botanists make mistakes. Or they learn new things about plants that help to categorize them better, such as the fact that the leaves of plants, like certain philodendrons, may change shape as they mature—so what was once considered a different species may be the same species, but in a different life stage. In these cases, I'll use the most up-to-date Latin name as defined by peer-reviewed science journals and The Plant List (www.theplantlist.org), the latter of which is a collaboration between the Royal Botanic Gardens, Kew, and the Missouri Botanical Garden and serves as one of the more current working lists of all known plant species.

Scientific names generally comprise a genus and a species name. A *genus* (or *genera* in the plural) is a taxonomic group consisting of one or more species. A *species* identifies a group of individuals that share key characteristics but are separate from other members of the genus. Botanical Latin names are typically italicized, with the genus capitalized and the species in lowercase—for instance, *Peperomia fraseri*, the scientific name of a plant commonly known as "flowering peperomia." If a specific species is unknown or unspecified, this is denoted by "sp." after the genus, for example, *Peperomia* sp.

Aside from the scientific mumbo jumbo, you'll also notice that before we get to the "how" of doing things, we'll first seek out the "why." I've always found that exploring the inner reaches of why things are the way they are allows me to have a much more intimate understanding of the plants I've chosen to surround myself with, which I believe have equally chosen to surround me.

Finally, you'll notice that the book is knitted together with personal stories—both from me and from the greater community of people who have brought plants into their lives. It's my hope that these firsthand experiences will help you picture the joy of growing, learning about, and living with and around plants. There's so much for us to learn from plants. As you'll find out, plants are always communicating in their own way. We just have to remember how to listen.

—SUMMER RAYNE OAKES

HOW TO
MAKE A PLANT
LOVE YOU

INTRODUCTION

I do not yet know why plants come out of the land or float in
streams, or creep on rocks or roll from the sea. I am entranced
by the mystery of them, and absorbed by their variety and
kinds. Everywhere they are visible yet everywhere occult.

—Liberty Hyde Bailey

. . . .

*"Plants calm me. As soon as I started to acquire plants
for my space, it's as if a light switch turned on and made me realize
that I had been in the dark this whole time. I can't tell you why
it is so, but that it just is." —Tomas*

F or years, I've wanted to write a book on plants. I spent much of my childhood outdoors. In the spring and summer, I would run through the timothy (*Phleum pratense*), fondly known as "tickle your ass grass," and emerge with streaks of spittlebug froth and red marks from the abrasive, silica-containing fescue (*Festuca arundinacea*) and ryegrass (*Lolium perenne*) on my bare, sun-kissed legs. In the colder months of autumn, I exulted in the brilliant shades of crimson, umber, and gold-flecked leaves that transfigured the landscape. And in the winter months, when my mittened hands turned up chunks of alabaster snow, I'd often find myself dazzled by emerald mosses snuggled cozy and unperturbed under their igloo homes on the forest floor.

It's difficult to put into words how alive I feel when I'm outside, among all the intricacies and mysteries of the natural world. I've spent much of my professional life connecting people back to nature. In time, my career path led me to New York City, where I had to retire my bug net and boots and largely trade in the lifestyle that I was accustomed to. I made this sacrifice in order to explore how urban people might reconnect to their environment through the products they consume regularly, like clothes, cosmetics, and food, and the actions that they take on a daily basis, like preparing and eating more locally sourced food (more on that later). Since I could no longer step out my back door and be immersed in nature, I needed to find a way to bring nature to me. I had to learn how to carve out my own personal green space in my apartment and in my community in the city, which meant cultivating an entirely new kind of relationship with plants in an entirely different context.

And so I began. I started with a fiddle-leaf fig (*Ficus lyrata*) in my bedroom over ten years ago now. Leaf by leaf, frond by frond, flower by flower, my indoor collection of green companions grew. I found plants by the side of the road, in long-forgotten window boxes, at farmers' markets and local garden shops, and even sprouting bravely between cracked pavement. Many found a home with me. I nestled them in sturdy terra-cotta pots, pretty cachepots, kitchen colanders (great drainage!), woven baskets, Mason jars, and rows of upcycled empty tea tins. I came up with inexpensive, inventive ways and places to shelve, hang, tuck, anchor, secure, and suspend them, circumventing the number and narrowness of my windowsills and pressing walls, poles, pillars, beams, and even a street-found trellis into service. In time, I had well over 1,000 plants and around 550 species and cultivars that took up residence in my home, which one of my friends accordingly dubbed "The Hanging Gardens of Brooklyn."

It appeared that my efforts touched a chord. I was shocked when my very verdant apartment went viral. Within months, tens of millions of people were watching videos or sharing stories on the plants in my home. Were they just looking for the gee-whiz story of the day? I don't think so. "Woman Lives with Hundreds of Houseplants" may be a compelling headline, but I sensed that there was more behind people's interest. Nor were they just looking for interior-design inspiration. I've learned that plants offer us far more than drool-worthy decor. And indeed, countless people have sent me stories—some of which you'll read in this book—of how their communion with plants has improved their lives in innumerable ways:

> "I love the cleaner air in my living room. The color my plants add to my home makes me feel noticeably happier. I live in a basement apartment with no windows, so I was thrilled that my plants could thrive in lightbulb light."
> —Alamay

> "My husband and I love having plants. The air feels cleaner, and seeing them on the windowsill when we wake up is soothing. Caring for them and watering them makes me feel calm and purposeful, as if I am succeeding in some small way. When they flower and bloom or just grow larger, I feel that I, too, am growing. And nourishing them with natural fertilizer helps me remember that I need to nourish myself."
> —Sarah A. @clandestine_thylacine

> "I find being in an area full of plants has an energy that is thick with the smell of greenery and the air makes me feel very refreshed. Tending my plants relaxes my mind. I slow down as I look for leaves to prune, and when I water them, it reminds me that they have their own schedule. When I'm with my plants, life feels nice and gentle."
> —Madeline T.

"I always thought I couldn't keep plants alive—that I had a black thumb. When my son was born, I had a horribly traumatic birth experience and developed postpartum depression that brought me to a pretty dark place. I started growing plants at the suggestion of a friend who is a horticultural therapist. Learning to care for plants, to notice them and see them thrive, gave me the confidence to see that my child was thriving, too." —Liz

"When I find myself getting anxious, I need to do something kinesthetic in order to distract my thoughts. Usually I repot my houseplants and untangle their roots, making sure they have space to grow and breathe. I also just sit with them and study their unique foliage. Sometimes I draw what I see. I lie in the sun with them during the day for a few minutes, and it reminds me to breathe more deeply." —Ivy

What is consistently striking in the messages people in my community send me is how far removed many of us seem to be from the outdoors, and how gratifying it is when we finally find our way back to nature and plants. So, why don't more of us?

Probably because the task seems daunting or impossible without a major lifestyle shift. Gardening, as we have known it, has not kept step with society's exodus from the countryside to city centers. Most of us don't have a patch of fertile dirt to call our own.

And yet the experience I had growing up of being immersed in plants is within our reach—including those of us living in tiny apartments in cities, those who know nothing about plants, those who believe they're too busy to take care of anything, never thought of themselves as nature types, or are convinced they have a "black thumb." I've found shortcuts, work-arounds, mind-sets, and strategic habits that you can use to bring plants and their life-giving qualities to you—no matter where you live and what your experience level is. In doing so, you'll not only learn how to bring plants into your life and keep them alive but also discover how to participate in an emotive human-plant dialogue that may impart invaluable lessons about yourself and your place here on Earth.

Though this is a book about plants, you may be surprised to hear that *How to Make a Plant Love You* is not strictly a gardening book. It's actually more of a relationship book. Plants, whether we know it or not, have been an integral part of our lives since we were born. In many cases, we may not even notice them; or if we do, we may acknowledge them as only interesting background objects or a pretty part of our decor. However, at the risk of sounding obvious, plants are living, breathing beings that when acknowledged and brought more intentionally into our lives, can be monumentally rewarding. Learning to live with plants and developing a relationship with them are goals that any motivated person can achieve—but just as fostering a strong, healthy, and rewarding relationship with another human being is not done by "care tips" alone, neither is a relationship with plants. Solid, lifelong, and rewarding relationships require a healthy dose of observation, respect, effort, understanding, and love—all of which we'll cover in this book.

Rest assured, I will be sharing advice on how to better care for your plants, too. But becoming skilled at plant care is only one of the benefits I hope you will gain from this book. Learning to be a good plant steward can lead to an even greater end. For at its very core, this is a book about how we can develop everyday skills and meaningful rituals that can positively affect our lives—and how we can further develop healthier, stronger relationships with ourselves, our community, and our home here on Earth—through our relationship with plants. And not only the plants that we choose to keep company with in our homes but also the ones that we may forget to notice in the world around us: the tough weeds surviving against all odds in the crooked crack of a sidewalk . . . the plants in the community garden down the block, lovingly tended by local volunteers . . . the trees of great, enigmatic forests that seem to exist as a fairy tale in our mind's eye, a distant memory stored deep and damp in our very DNA—a reminder that at some point, we all were sprung from Mother Nature's earthy womb.

Throughout this book, I map out the course of our migration as a society away from plants and our re-embracement of them in our lives, albeit in new and different ways. Additionally, I challenge you to broaden your view of plants and encourage you to look at life a little more from a plant's perspective. What we discover is that as we get to know plants a little better, we become more in touch with ourselves, and through that self-awareness and observation become not only better at caring for plants but also better caretakers of ourselves, the people around us, and our planet. So, let's step inside the world of plants and discover how we can begin cultivating our own personal green space—in our homes, in our minds, and in our hearts.

1

THE MASS MIGRATION

You didn't come into this world. You came out of it,
like a wave from the ocean. You are not a stranger here.

—*Alan Watts*

· · · · · · · · · ·

*"Plants are beautiful and unique. They grow the way
they want, without any pressure to grow the way someone
else wants them to grow. I use my plants to see life more clearly.
To understand that it can be simple." —Sarah Solange*

I t was preposterous to think I'd ever live in a city. All that concrete and glass piled on top of one another, the loud noises, the starless sky. I bet the frogs I put carefully in buckets to bring home as a kid would never have guessed that I would ever leave the countryside, either.

I PADDED DOWN the forest path, my feet light and quick. I had read somewhere, or maybe I heard it from a childhood friend, that Native Americans who had lived and hunted in Pennsylvania were so silent that when they ran in the woods, they could barely be detected by animal or enemy. I marveled at that idea. And aspired to be as silent.

It was easier to travel quietly in the morning, after a heavy dew, or just after a rain. The sounds of the forest floor were dampened then, and that's often when birdsong would be at its highest. I whooshed past the hemlocks, inhaling their lemony pine scent. Wet ferns tickled my shins with their feather touch. The forest floor glinted with emerald mats of mosses and the waxy, evergreen leaves of creepers: partridgeberry (*Mitchella repens*) and wintergreen

(*Gaultheria procumbens*). Once in a while something would catch my eye that required a closer inspection: a flower I hadn't noticed before, a dew-laden insect creeping along the underside of a leaf, or a bright-orange jelly fungus oozing from the wound of a fallen tree branch. I'd collect it if I wanted to continue studying it. Then I would clamber over the stone wall that bridled the forest from our freshly mowed lawn.

I would often press plants between books, arrange them in indoor mini-habitats akin to dioramas, and commandeer parts of the refrigerator for my science experiments. Before I turned five, I absconded with my brother's never-used birthday present—a beautifully designed, German-made microscope, which came equipped with captivating glass slides mounted with thinly sliced onion skins, moss-leaf cells, and diatoms and a box of empty slides that I could make myself. I put it to good use for nearly a decade of my childhood. Even today I lust for a well-made microscope, as it's a superb way to bring us closer to nature—literally and figuratively.

I learned to love the forest and everything in it. So much so that it was often challenging for my parents to get me to come home. In my teenage years, I was content to spend most of every summer day in the woods, rarely seeing my school friends. But I never once felt alone.

In addition to learning to love the wildness of nature, I grew up seeing the beautiful communion that can happen when humans and plants cooperate. Outside the forest, my mother prided herself on the upkeep of her immaculate flower gardens. Bright yellow forsythias (*Forsythia* × *intermedia*), which shone like sunbeams in spring, bordered our land; double-flowered hollyhocks (*Alcea* sp.) in whites, pinks, and wines stood as erect as the Queen's Guard out of the rockiest of soils; gaily dressed tulips (*Tulipa* sp.) and daylilies (*Hemerocallis* sp.)—in the colors of an African sunset—were impressively plentiful; the musky scent of marigolds (*Tagetes* sp.) and Queen Anne's lace (*Daucus carota*) would be all too apparent if you cared to bend down to weed; and the smell of hyacinths, lilacs, and pillow-soft peonies (*Hyacinthus* sp., *Syringa* sp., *Paeonia* sp.) the size of pink cabbages filled the air and coated the back of your throat with the most intoxicating perfumes.

The vegetable garden and orchard, tended by both my mother and father, were equally impressive. At just a half an acre, the land had enough delights to please the senses, like the pucker-your-face tartness of rhubarb stalks (*Rheum rhabarbarum*) and shiny redcurrants (*Ribes rubrum*), which my mother would make pies and crepes with, respectively. Or how could I forget my favorite foraged flavor—the gooseberry (*Ribes hirtellum*), whose russet-colored flesh and pectinous bite were like eating a sweet-but-tart grape? It was within this cultivated space that I learned the lessons of patience, respect, and trust in the internal clocks of living things. Plants thrive when provided with the conditions to reach their potential in their own time. In the beginning of the season, we would transport pungent composted cow dung from my aunt's farm next door and generously spread it over the land until it was nearly shin deep. The strawberries, squash, cucumbers, asparagus, lettuce, melons, peas, beans, and tomatoes loved it, and we always had far more fruits and vegetables during the growing season than our family of four could eat. There was always the fun of waiting for the next seasonal crop to burst forth, or wondering if the raspberries would be as plentiful this season as the last. Anticipating their bounty seemed to heighten my curiosity in the plants we were growing.

Maybe the sweetness of anticipation is the reason I still eat seasonally as much as possible, often making a pilgrimage to my local greenmarket on Saturdays to purchase fresh fruits and vegetables for my weekly meals (and to drop off my composted food waste, produced from my previous week's purchases). Somehow the intentionality of this ritual connects me to a timeline more far-reaching and unrushable than the twenty-four-hour clock we're all caught up in.

Back home in my plant-filled apartment, I love preparing a meal among the ample leafage, which gives me a sense of "camping" indoors. Even in the winter months, when everything outside in the cold northeast seems gray and dour, most of my plants indoors still exhibit much vitality and life—even flaunting a rogue bloom here or there, which is always a treat. Last winter, my *Kleinia fulgens,* also known as coral senecio or scarlet kleinia, pleasantly surprised me with a profusion of carmine-colored pom-poms, a starkly beautiful contrast against its subdued, gray-green leaves and the frosted windows behind. Once you start your plant pilgrimage, you may find that this affirmation of bud and bloom helps you savor the long-term relationship you've been developing with your plant, particularly after months of a little daily TLC.

My parents, speaking of TLC, were in the garden regularly—clearing the weeds, picking the zucchini, or cutting back the asparagus or garlic, two plants that seemed to spread spontaneously once established. I got the sense from my folks that there was much to do, but it wasn't onerous. If anything, it was just as natural to be in the garden as it was to eat the fruits of our labor at the dinner table. In fact, the entire process seemed to be a joy. Hands in dirt was a way of life, and there was much to relish in those unembellished rituals.

The cultivation of flowers and veggies interested me, but I was most attracted to the wild plants strewn throughout the lawn and forest—and even as unwelcome migrants in the garden beds. They seemed to be the outsiders: unrestrained and unmanicured, prolific and unpretentious. They were all so different, packed tightly in and up against one another, yet they all seemed to cohabit unexpectedly well. In hindsight, it's how I like my plants even when I bring them indoors—wild, unrestrained, a little unkempt, and surprisingly collaborative. They've taught me a great deal about how those who at first appear rowdy, pushy, and willful can be appreciated for their vitality, vigor, and persistence, if their nature is well understood and treated with kindness and caring boundaries.

I also learned, from poring over the thick, yellowing pages of my mother's 1974 copy of *The Rodale Herb Book*, that nearly all the plants around me could be used to heal, soothe, and nourish. Plants like coltsfoot (*Tussilago farfara*), purslane (*Portulaca oleracea*), and soapwort (*Saponaria officinalis*) were no longer weeds to be pulled, but plants to be studied. I would play pharmacist, cook, and chemist—boiling coltsfoot leaves, noshing on purslane, and mashing up the leaves of the soapwort to release the bubbly saponins from which it gets its name. Even before there was fancy lab equipment to isolate plant alkaloids and scents, someone had taken notice; someone had observed and experimented with plants to uncover unique properties such as those. The secret healing and other potential powers of nature are there for the knowing. We just have to be willing to look for them.

It wasn't easy to leave those beautiful woods, fields, orchards, and gardens. I moved to New York City to work. It's where I envisioned experimenting with life and reaching my "fullest potential"—at least from a professional standpoint. And the work I've done here would have been far more difficult to attempt living back home in the country. I spent around fifteen years in the world of fashion, produced films, and engaged in the startup scene with my own businesses. Working with other creatives and entrepreneurs, living a fast-paced life in the city, I discovered that reaching one's "fullest potential" often involves some trade-offs.

I remember hearing on a radio report as a kid in the nineties that in just a short period of time, more people on the planet would live in cities, outnumbering those residing in rural and suburban areas. Sure enough, about ten years ago, that prediction of mass migration became a reality: In the United States, nearly 81 percent of the general population now lives in urban areas, including me. And of the general population, 66 percent of us "Millennials"—or people born between 1980 and 2000, according to many psychologists—have flocked to cities and outlying metropolitan areas like winged insects feverishly encircling street lamps at dusk. As a result, for the first time since the 1920s, growth in US cities outpaces growth outside of them. And today, 55 percent of the world's population considers urban centers home—a statistic projected to grow an additional 13 percentage points by 2050. This means that cities small and large are rapidly expanding, at least partially due to my own generation's move to them.

Countless studies and opinions have already been circulated about Millennial trends. We live differently than previous generations. We're more likely to delay marriage because we want to linger in the beatitude of singledom. We also delay mortgages—not because we don't want to own our own homes, but largely because we can't afford the expense, particularly if we're eyeing the real estate in our beloved cities. But none of these trends explains our exodus from some of our more spacious, idyllic birthplaces.

My friends cite a few key reasons for their migrations: more people, more ideas, more innovations. In the city, you can create and reinvent yourself over and over again. It's a pulsing human-centric ecosystem. Opportunities often come about by being in a place, meeting people, and putting yourself out there. Theoretically that happens more in cities because, like the charged electrons of the sun, we bump into each other more often. And you want more of these opportunities because when you come of the professional age when "having to make a living" (as opposed to plain "living") becomes a mandate, you need to make some clear-eyed choices about going where the work is. And if you have to make some trade-offs in the process, so be it.

I often say it would be wonderful to have a backyard again. Dare I even hope for a forest to stroll in? I stopped by one of my local plant stores and shared that I was looking at a place upstate with a little land. The young woman behind the register sighed. "That's everyone's dream who works here." Granted, I was with people who probably love being out in nature, and I realize not everyone feels that way, but I know many of us do. Before college I never expected to move to the city—and once I did, I never foresaw that I would be in the city for so long. But my longing for space, for nature, and for those quiet blessings that come with it had to be pushed aside for other pursuits that I deemed more vitally important than a vegetable garden.

The trade-offs don't always stop with relocation. The search for work satisfaction, alongside life satisfaction, is a tandem quest many of us pursue whether we moved to a city or not. Many of my peers have left their positions because the work wasn't fulfilling or engaging. A 2016 Gallup poll corroborates this: 71 percent of Millennials are either disengaged or not engaged at work, which makes us the least-engaged generation in the United States. This disengagement results in frequent job hunting and switching. Millennials are changing jobs far more than previous generations, with one report showing that they are three times more likely to leave their current workplace than workers of other generations. Though other reports show that the difference is not that dramatic, the long-term trend reveals that we're definitely changing our jobs more than our parents and grandparents did at our age, with the added pressures of less-secure jobs with longer hours.

These statistics may imply that Millennials leave their jobs with the greatest of ease, but from my experience, this is not the case. "Career change" is one of the main topics of discussion in meditation and discussion circles with friends. And nearly all of my friends who have changed jobs—or who have left jobs and are seeking a new career—feel a high degree of uneasiness, uncertainty, stress, and even guilt.

Add to all of this the fact that most of us live busy lives—so busy that we barely give ourselves the permission to pause. When we do, we socialize on the go and not necessarily in person. We've replaced social time with time on social media—over 90 percent of us use it, and research shows we spend hours a day scrolling, commenting, and liking. Yes, social media can be very useful (my advice: limit yourself to groups that focus on stuff you're into—like plants—and stop just scrolling your feeds), but studies have shown that it's also a depressant. A large-scale 2016 study of young adults aged nineteen to thirty-two revealed that participants using multiple social media platforms had substantially higher odds of having increased levels of both depression and anxiety symptoms. Never before in human history have we been able to see and know so much stuff. That can be great when doing research on our favorite subject, but it's otherwise not so great for us emotionally. Furthermore, FOMO—or the "fear of missing out"—drives us to expand our world of people whose lives we can only glimpse, making it easy to think our lives are inferior. The curated, unrealistic imagery associated with social feeds can lead to what my friend Nitika Chopra refers to as "compare and despair syndrome."

If we're substituting social media for face-to-face friends, and multitasking between multiple platforms—in the midst of actual work time or family time—is it any wonder we're more anxious than ever before? New research shows that my generation in general spends nearly one-sixth of the year feeling stressed-out. And about 67 percent of us—significantly more than previous generations—say financial stress not only overtakes our ability to focus and be productive at work but also takes a toll on our health.

Our financial stress may be partly due to the fact that, even though we're a more educated generation, today's graduates on average carry the burden of over $37,000 in student loans. A 2014 Gallup poll shows that graduates who have over $50,000 in debt are less likely than nonborrowers to be thriving in four of five areas, including purpose and financial, community, and physical well-being. And to top this off, 33 percent of young adults in the United States, primarily in their twenties, are living with their parents or grandparents, largely to "save up" because they're either working a less-than-adequate job or still pursuing one. It's tough to say whether debt is causing emotional fallout or whether these challenges are simply coexisting, but from anecdotal reports with peers and those who are getting ready to graduate, the pain—or shall I say the stress—is real.

Finding balance amid the chaos is essential. Luckily, many of us have developed healthy and sensible strategies to reduce stress and anxiety—from meditation to fitness routines. Though working out or having a meditation practice can be done alone, group workouts and meditation sessions have become ever more popular, allowing us to form the beginnings of a nonwork community.

These are all positive strides. But while we are masters at connecting through our devices and through our expansive networks, many of us are disconnected from the natural world, even though we intuitively know that quality time outdoors and being in the presence of plants provide balance, energy, and calm. There is some evidence that we're trying to remedy that. According to the 2016 National Gardening Survey, 6 million people started gardening inside or outdoors that year. Of those, 5 million were Millennials. Closer to home, the fact that my own plant predilections have generated so much interest across so many groups buoys my hope that we are taking steps to bring more balance into our lives by increasing our connection with nature. Whatever age or stage you're at in life, this book will help you reach that goal.

Let me assure you that you don't have to quit your job, pack your bags, and move to the forest—though I'm not advocating against it, particularly if it's where your calling is! But there are myriad more practical ways to connect to the natural world and become enriched and grounded in the present moment. Taking just a little bit of time out of the day to acknowledge and observe plants, for instance, is a simple but powerful way to become more centered and aware—a technique I'll share shortly. And as I've learned through intuition, interest, and experience, bringing plants into my life has allowed me to feel rooted in a city that did not at first feel like my home. Through cultivating my own personal green space, I have been able to make New York City very much my home. I want you to experience the beauty, tranquility, and joy that being in the company of plants can provide—whether it's just a charming little succulent waving its plump ciabatta arms at you each morning from your studio apartment windowsill; a motley gaggle of kitchen herbs that cheerfully contribute fresh basil leaves to zest up your salads, sprigs of rosemary to season roasted potatoes, and stomach-soothing mint for your tea; or maybe, if you're up for it, your own lovingly chosen version of the home jungle I adore.

But cultivating your personal green space can be about so much more than just buying a bunch of plants from your garden center to adorn your windowsill, balcony, or (lucky you!) backyard. To really forge a relationship with the plants that will become a part of your life, the first step is simply to shift your mind-set. In this book, I'll teach you how to make the world of plants—sometimes right under your nose, but not noticed until now—open up to you. This small shift can enrich your life as you take in the quiet dignity of plants doing their thing, valiantly rooting and growing and budding and blooming and shedding, sometimes under pretty dire conditions; quietly and efficiently cleaning and replenishing the very air we breathe; and thriving all around you. I'll show you how to develop skills that, if practiced, will stay with you forever and allow you to reap the fullest rewards that the presence of plants has to offer. When you combine your ability to understand the needs of plants with the fundamentals I will teach you here, you will have not only beautiful plants to enrich your life but also an education and perspective you can take with you wherever you move in the world.

"At a dark time in my life, my seven-year relationship ended, I left my job, and I found myself alone. My best friend brought me my first succulent for my tiny new bare apartment. It sat in my window in my bedroom. Slowly I built up my collection of plants, learned more about them, their specific needs for sun, water, and soil, and have strived to help every one flourish. I have propagated that first little plant probably almost a hundred times and given succulent starts to many people. It's so therapeutic for me to think that the plant that kept me hanging on is now passing pieces of itself on to others. It gives me a very clear picture of how love and light can spread throughout the world."
—Sarah C.

"To refer to plant care as a hobby diminishes the reality of what plants hold. Plants harness a constellation of powers that invite the intellect and incite the soul. On their surface they may simply please the eye, but beneath their stillness they hide a magnitude of depth and contradiction. They await and yearn for understanding. They strive, like any breathing being, to thrive, rather than to merely exist. This task is hardly simple. Plants evolve alongside an evolution in our perceptions. When we work to instill life into a plant, it may too instill life within us."
—Chris Siriphand

GET-GROWING EXERCISE: REFLECTION

1. Did you have any exposure to plants or gardening while growing up? If so, what were some of your most memorable experiences? If these experiences happened later in life, reflect on those. If they have yet to happen, what are your ideas to encourage more communing with plants, gardening, or nature?

2. Did any particular person or people in your life influence or foster your interest in plants? How so?

3. How do you think your attitude toward plants has changed as you have matured?

2

OUR NEED FOR NATURE

**Our task is not to return to Nature in the manner of
Rousseau, but to find the natural man again.**

—C. G. Jung

. . . .

*"When I'm with my plants, I forget all about work, college,
and responsibility. For some reason I can be fully myself. Also,
to keep something alive and healthy feels amazing. I feel like
a positive person who can help and provide. I can believe in
myself in my little forest." —Tasneem Saad Alenezi*

ur plane slid into Singapore during the early-morning hours. A soft haze, either smog from forests burning in Indonesia or just a hazy cloud cover, hung in the air. I grabbed my carry-ons and picked the crust from my right eye to catch a good glimpse of the outdoors, but the fog was impenetrable.

I rolled off the plane and into a visual fusillade of foliage. I breathed deeply as my senses, dulled by twelve hours in the recycled air of a cramped airplane cabin, absorbed the spacious hallways, the sky-high ceilings, and a textured sea of green at Changi Airport.

The hallways of Changi Airport are wallpapered with botanical art, but they also practically burst at the seams with living plants. Origami pockets on the wall provide homes for shaggy *Dracaena* sp., *Philodendron* sp., *Monstera* sp., and *Epipremnum* sp. The baggage-claim area features an interior island teeming in *Phalaenopsis* sp., *Anthurium* sp., and *Neoregelia* sp., a colorful bromeliad. The lounges are resplendent with dense but well-manicured towering palms, fuchsia *Cordyline* sp., and a range of other tropical plants.

Though I arrived at the airport at 7 AM, I didn't leave until three hours later, partly because the airline had lost my luggage, but also in part because I wasn't in any rush to go. I was more than happy to get an early lunch and sit beneath the palms in the lounge while I waited for my luggage to find me. How many airports can you say that about?

But the greening of Singapore goes far beyond the airport. Singapore has become a houseplant lover's mecca—a sort of Disneyland of Horticultural Wonderment, a plant lover's wet dream. Anyone who remains unconvinced that plants can positively affect one's life just needs to talk to any Singaporean, because "living with plants" has become deeply encultured in their day-to-day lives. Even my former plant-disinterested college roommate, Ray, messaged me to bring him "an exotic air plant from the United States," as he had become crazy about *Tillandsia* sp. and had amassed a collection that he was thoroughly excited to show me. He even gave me a few tips on the best places to plant shop.

Though Singapore—just 88 miles (141.6 kilometers) due north of the equator with a relative humidity in the 70 to 80 percent range—may be a tad too uncomfortable for humans, it's Nirvana for tropical plants, which seem to bask on buildings with the greatest of ease. As you walk the streets of Singapore, you are almost always within eyeshot of some pleasing green space.

Even as I emerged to street level from one of Singapore's subterranean train stations in search of my hotel, all I had to do was look up: the Oasia Hotel Downtown, which was named Best Tall Building Worldwide by the Council on Tall Buildings and Urban Habitat in 2018, features sixty stories of green walls, which envelop its red steel exterior from top to bottom with a most alluring ensemble of clambering *Epipremnum* sp., *Thunbergia* sp., *Passiflora* sp., and

Bauhinia sp. Inside, open-air terraces offer communal green space, featuring towering *Ficus lyrata* and *Clusia rosea*, comprising over 40 percent of the building's volume. That's a surprising amount of open space for a building where real estate prices come at a premium, but there's an increasing—almost obsessive—trend by the government and private businesses to maximize quality of life for citizens and patrons, respectively. Plants, it turns out, are one way to do that.

Singapore wasn't always this green. I first visited the island city-state in 2005, the same year that "the Gardens by the Bay," a 250-acre nature park with otherworldly architectural design and hundreds of thousands of plants, was being conceptualized. This, along with the Republic's 300 parks and four nature reserves, was one of the many initiatives helping to rebrand Singapore from a "Garden City" to "a City in a Garden" and has catapulted it to the top of cities boasting urban leafage. In a way, Gardens by the Bay encapsulates the city's larger vision, with its Flower Dome and Cloud Forest, the latter featuring colossal green walls, a 115-foot (35-meter) waterfall, and a skyway dotted with throngs of slack-jawed tourists. "When I saw the 3-D renderings of Gardens by the Bay," said Chad Davis, assistant director of conservatory operations for the gardens, "it felt like a scene out of *Avatar*. This helped put Singapore on the map . . . and now we are a model for the world. I think Gardens by the Bay shows the interest of the government and the effort they're willing to put into greening up the city. They funded us to get us up to opening, and when they talk about greening Singapore, they are serious."

At the time of its independence, Singapore, a country nearly the size of New York City and half the size of London, had around

1.9 million inhabitants. Now, over fifty years later, that number has nearly tripled to a population of almost 5.7 million, making it the second-densest nation-state in the world. Singapore, which juts out at the end of the Malay Peninsula, has become heavily urbanized in order to keep pace with its burgeoning population and booming economy. Not one to be constrained by its watery bounds as an island, Singapore has begun to fill in the natural swamps and estuaries to build land, an environmentally controversial process called "reclamation," as the city is "reclaiming" land from the watery grip of the sea. Since its independence, it has increased its land mass by a remarkable 22 percent. In the process, unfortunately, it had to destroy much of its natural environment. Population growth in Singapore has remained relatively stable, but it will continue, with the population expected to reach around 6 million by 2020. One would think that the Republic's response to the increase in population would be to add more buildings, not green space. But a multidecade initiative from the government has insisted on integrating plants—both native and nonnative—back into the landscape, be it on car parks or buildings, or even as floating wetlands on waterways and reservoirs.

What spurred the sudden interest in greenery? And in what specific ways is it good for us to be close to nature? Turns out that Singapore, like many urban areas, is particularly prone to urban heat island (often referred to as UHI) effect, a phenomenon that happens when human activities and man-made structures replace vegetation, which formerly provided evaporative cooling. During certain times of the day, built areas can be more than 7°C (45°F) hotter than more rural areas, which leads to spiked energy use (and therefore pollution) by indoor environments and, outdoors contributes to a person's discomfort and affects overall well-being. I spoke with Conrad Heinz Philipp, senior researcher and project coordinator of Cooling Singapore, a consortium of universities, research scientists, and agencies funded by the government to tackle this issue and come up with the best long-term strategy for the country's heat problem. As part of their work, they have collected more than eighty mitigation strategies to increase human comfort in tropical climates, and they began doing field research with residents and passersby in the residential district of Punggol. "People are really into greenery and shaded places instead of having more artificial cooling strategies, like cool bus stations," he shared with me over a Skype call. When people were asked to rank mitigation strategies in order of preference, "green streetscapes" and "green facades" ranked number one and number two—making vegetation the preference of those interviewed.

Though a more robust cost analysis of planting and maintaining green streetscapes and facades still needs to be undertaken, the Singaporean government has not postponed greening efforts, seeming to pay heed to the proverb: "The best time to plant a tree was twenty years ago. The second-best time is now." This proactive approach has paid off. Through its greening efforts, Singapore has been able to show a plethora of benefits, including that green areas not only can significantly reduce heat in the city by up to 4.5°C (40°F) but also, in the case of plants on a building's facade, can increase the comfort of people both indoors and outdoors—and perhaps most importantly, can delight, engage, and bring joy to the city's inhabitants.

Singapore exemplifies some of the many benefits that can be found on a macro level when a city decides it needs plants. But while we wait for most cities to get the memo, individuals are discovering that they can create their own calming environments when they meet up with plants one on one.

One of the plant nurseries I visited in Singapore was Terrascapes. When I arrived, I was met by a barrage of bird cackles from a colorful and quirky crew of cockatoos, conures, and caiques hanging out in the nursery. There I met Bridgette, who had begun working with Sandy, the owner of Terrascapes, just two years prior. She had visited the nursery in search of succulents that she wouldn't kill, and while discussing plant care with Sandy, she saw an opportunity for them to help one another. Plants weren't her specialty, but she grew up on a quail farm where her parents grew all their own food. "As a kid we rarely ever went to the market to buy vegetables. We just ate whatever we could harvest," she told me. "It was just part of my life that I never really paid attention to."

That was until she decided to leave behind her high-profile job as a leading optometrist and her side ventures, which included running a café and a charity. Around eight years ago, Bridgette began developing symptoms of an autoimmune disorder, which likely stemmed from a combination of constant stress and being sick without proper treatment. "I was always rushing around," she admitted. "I couldn't sleep, and then I began developing chronic pain and depression." She figured she just needed a break and some time off. But after taking three months off, she was not improving. "The pain was still there. When I went to get blood tests, the doctor told me that my whole body was inflamed."

Bridgette began a slow retreat from her high-stress professional life. She started spending more time with her parents and noticed what a green thumb her mother had. That made her want to try growing some succulents herself, which is how she first came upon Terrascapes. Sandy's nursery appealed to her because, unlike most nurseries in the area, which buy plants outside the country for resale, Sandy tends to grow many of his plants from seeds or cuttings. What had started as a visit to a plant store to buy a plant or two for her home became an opportunity to assuage her condition and assist Sandy in the process. She asked if she could potentially help him in the greenhouse, and he was more than happy to bring her on board. "Propagating plants and watching them grow is most satisfying," Bridgette shared. "It keeps me wanting to come back and do more. Plus, I like getting my hands dirty. It seems to help me feel really good when I do. For the life of me I cannot meditate, but getting my hands dirty, weeding plants—it somehow feels meditative. I can do it for hours and hours." Plants, in some small way, allowed Bridgette to be productive again.

Like Bridgette, Mauritian-born James Ipy also uses plants for therapeutic purposes. When he was in his early teens, a neighbor passed along an *Adiantum capillus-veneris*, a maidenhair fern with thin paw-shaped leaflets and delicate, wiry black stems. This simple gesture in turn helped stoke his love for plants. He later moved to Singapore for work and boasts one of the best small balcony gardens around. "I specifically got this place for its balcony so I can grow plants," he confessed to me when I came over to ogle his beautiful ferns and huperzias, the latter of which hung like soft green tassels from a makeshift wire strung like a clothesline across the balcony ceiling to increase space for plants.

"I work in IT," he told me, "and if I didn't have plants, I don't know what I would do. They're like therapy for me. No matter how bad a day I've had at work, the moment I get home every evening, I open my door and see my garden and all my troubles are left behind. Knowing that my plants depend on me and thrive under my care is comforting and therapeutic. Tending to them literally keeps me sane."

Turning to plants in an urban context to feel calm and collected seems to be a healthy response. But some rapidly urbanizing areas that don't have access to greenery, like other cities throughout Asia, are beginning to report on cases in children of "biophobia," a phenomenon in which people who are not exposed to nature become reluctant, fearful, or anxious when outdoors. In some cases, "biophobic" people are reluctant to even put their hands in soil. Singapore's response is admirable: Today, about a third of the country's 278.5 square miles (721.3 square kilometers) is covered by greenery, with about 3 million trees in streetscapes, parks, and residential areas and on rooftops and balconies. In addition, 300 kilometers, or 186 miles, of green paths and corridors now connect the parks, and currently over 80 percent of people live within ten minutes of a green space.

Back home in New York, we're decidedly less green. Granted, it's partially due to our latitude: not much but ivy will grow on our walls through the wintertime, but despite that seasonal handicap, over the past ten years—at least in and around my neighborhood—there's been a slow- but steady-growing expanse of parks, green roofs, and secret gardens. My own community garden is a wonderful hidden getaway from the city—a good place to unwind.

As with Singapore, there's a good reason why there are more green spaces in NYC than when I moved in nearly fourteen years ago—and it's not just because gardens are pretty or increase property values. Studies have shown that these islands of green in our cities, whether manicured parks, urban forests, or even an alleyway converted to a community garden, are great for residents' mental health. One study found that these areas bring locals a 40 percent reduction in feeling depressed and a 50 percent reduction in feeling worthless. Green spaces also offer opportunities for people to enjoy wildlife sightings.

Even if you can't walk in a park every day, even a little exposure can help—countless research reports, mostly done with hospital patients, have shown that a room with a nature view or indoor plants helped reduce nervous, anxious, or tense feelings in study participants. Those fortunate enough to have a view of trees rather than a view of a building were found to use fewer pain-reducing medications and have quicker recovery times from surgery. Additionally, a smaller study has shown that transplanting an indoor plant more significantly reduces psychological and physiological stress as compared to doing a task on a computer. This calming effect is accomplished through the suppression of sympathetic nervous system activity[1] and blood pressure.

The realization that being around plants can heal has led to the formation of professions such as horticultural therapy, a discipline in which practitioners design programs of therapy and rehabilitation for people through plants, such as gardening activities and interaction with nature.

Matthew J. Wichrowski, MSW HTR, horticultural therapist, clinical assistant professor, and editor in chief of the *Journal of Therapeutic Horticulture*, began working in the field of horticultural therapy in 1991. After college, he had an opportunity to renovate an old

---

1 The sympathetic nervous system controls the body's response to a perceived threat, often known as the "fight or flight" response.

greenhouse and later help develop a program working with autistic adults in the greenhouse. "When I saw that many residents were much calmer in the greenhouse setting, I began doing some research and found out there was a community of folks working with nature," he shared with me. This eventually led him to work in the Enid A. Haupt Glass Garden at NYU Langone's Rusk Institute of Rehabilitation Medicine, where he now has been for twenty-five years.

The Glass Garden, a 1,700-square-foot (158-square-meter) greenhouse, had originally been designed as a retreat from the treatment center, but in the 1970s it was utilized to bring horticultural therapy into the medical setting. Unfortunately, both the garden and the hospital were heavily hit during Hurricane Sandy in 2012, so Matthew has improvised since then, bringing a flower and foliage cart bedside to patients. "Many of my patients bring the plant [of their choosing] home with them once they get out of the hospital," he told me. "It's important that they feel empowered and know how to care for them. . . . For some, it may be a boost of self-confidence."

Studies in horticultural therapy are becoming more prevalent as the relatively nascent field matures. One such study documented the effects of horticultural therapy programs on patients in cardiopulmonary rehabilitation. It was found that patients participating in horticultural programs had better mood states and reduced stress compared to the control group. Yet another therapeutic horticultural practitioner wrote to me of her firsthand experiences with clients:

> "I work primarily with older adults in assisted living and memory care communities, along with other groups like resettled refugees and individuals who rarely leave their

hospital beds. I use plants and gardening activities to improve their quality of life and overall well-being. It is remarkable to witness on a daily basis the various ways in which nature and plants provide respite and healing for individuals. I once worked with a client living with dementia who also had mobility issues and rarely spoke during our sessions—I had only heard him sing once, never talk, at that point. One day when gardening with the group outdoors in a raised bed, he stood up from his wheelchair (with assistance), picked up a soil cultivator, and started raking and tilling the soil by hand. As he planted, he started singing. Then he spoke, sharing stories about growing up on his father's farm and naming the crops they grew.

With another client who is a resettled refugee, during a lesson about trees and tree rings, she related some of her feelings about the challenges of being displaced from her native country and trauma she had experienced to the history of the tree whose rings we were studying: some years the tree thrived and grew a lot—just like she had during positive times in childhood—while in other years the tree endured challenges, like drought or fire or pest problems, and grew a little—as had happened to her during some of her experiences during war." —Susan Morgan

Matthew noted to me that horticultural therapy is increasingly being used to treat stress, in addition to special conditions like autism or dementia. Having just presented at conferences in the Nordic region, he shared that there is a prevalence of burnout

syndrome in those societies. "Horticultural therapy is being utilized to help folks return to work and become productive members
of society again. It's all-around great for promoting healthy lifestyle
and prevention." I hear from many people who have discovered the
stress-relieving power of plants:

> "I am an anxious person, and when alone with my thoughts
> I tend to feel overwhelmed and depressed. I've contem-
> plated therapy in the past but was always too afraid to go.
> Coincidentally, as I started taking an interest in plants, I
> found that I was less anxious because my mind focused on
> caring for the plants. For instance, I would work myself up
> thinking that my work, or what I've accomplished, isn't
> enough and would never be enough. I would often cry
> about this and ponder it daily. It would weigh down my
> partner and my family. I'm not sure how, but the more
> plants I had around me, the better I felt. It was as if
> something had lifted from my chest. I think the sense of
> completion started to come when I noticed how much my
> plants thrived under my care." —Nina

> "I'm a software developer. My work requires extended
> hours, and I often come home late. Three years ago, I
> started growing plants to cope with stress and with the
> death of my dog. It became a hobby. Now I follow groups
> on social media related to growing plants and have gained
> friends through that. Growing plants has helped me forget
> my worries and be able to save Mother Earth as well."
> —Maricar

"I work in the tech/retail industry. It's a fast-paced, sensory-overload environment that takes a lot out of me mentally, emotionally, and physically. I find it so relaxing and calming to tend to my plants. I water them, dust the leaves, check for bugs. It's gratifying when plants give me positive feedback right away with new growth or gorgeous blooms [it's] and interesting to watch them develop. Tending them gives me a sense of accomplishment and happiness. Sometimes I just gaze at my green corner—it helps to relax my eyes and mind." —@Plant_Jemima

This idea of using plants as a visual aid in healing and soothing people has been around for millennia, but perhaps seems novel or "new-agey" to us today—or maybe it has simply been overlooked or taken for granted. In Egypt, kings set aside extensive land for ecclesiastical tree temples for people to enjoy, and where students could come to study all of the medicinal and occult wonders that plants had to offer. In medieval Europe, monasteries created elaborate gardens to soothe those who were ill. And in the 1800s, it was not uncommon to see gardens and plants in both European and American hospitals for that same reason.

Now doctors throughout Asia are prescribing their high-anxiety urban dwellers a "forest bath"—known as *Shinrin-yoku* in Japan. This particular term was coined by the Japanese Ministry of Agriculture, Forestry, and Fisheries in 1982 and can be defined as making contact with and taking in the atmosphere of the forest. The doctors who prescribe this treatment usually suggest a short jaunt through the forest for a few days. I don't know about you, but my doctor never once prescribed that I "get outside more"—even when

I was low on vitamin D! The results of forest bathing on people's health is undeniable. People who were studied before and after *Shinrin-yoku* had lower levels of cortisol (the stress hormone); a lower pulse rate; lower blood pressure; greater parasympathetic nerve activity, which helps the body rest and digest; lower sympathetic nerve activity, which activates the "fight or flight" response in humans; increased immune function and response; and even more positive feelings than they did in their city environs.

But what if you have no forest at your doorstep? One way to restore that connection while living in the city is by bringing plants indoors. My houseplants stimulate my innate curiosity for other lifeforms, creating a calming environment in the city, providing a ritual of enjoyment, and keeping me in touch with what makes me feel whole. In a way, they keep me connected to what I love most and what makes me feel "at home" while serving as a reminder and an enabler to get outdoors and cherish the earth.

HOW ONE GREEN THUMB CAN CHANGE A COMMUNITY

In the book *Darkness and Daylight; or, Lights and Shadows of New York Life*, published in 1892, the author eloquently documents the powerful effects resulting from the simple yet visionary act of starting a humble garden in Corlear's Hook, an area on the East River of New

York, just across from where I live now. The area, described as "unknown ground to all save the police and
the gangs of thieves, murderers, and tramps that in-
fested . . . the squalid rookeries," became home for ten-
ement children. The partial reconstruction of the area,
according to the authors, started with plants. During a
walk through the slums, the founder of the Children's
Aid Society found an open-air building with sun on all
sides, for which he hired a superintendent who happened to have a love for plants and a particularly good
green thumb. The author describes in vivid detail what
happened next:

> The back yard—a mere strip of a place hardly big-
> ger than a respectable closet—was the first to
> yield to his magic touch. Here he planted shrubs,
> flowers, and vines about a shaded seat, where for
> a moment those who rested on it might fancy
> themselves in the country. Sewers and bilge-
> water were the best-known smells in this region,
> and he fought them with hyacinths and helio-
> trope and violets. In the school-room above, and
> through the lodging-house which was part of the
> mission of the building, plants and flowers were
> scattered about, unconsciously taming the rough
> little subjects who came in, and who begged for a
> single flower with an eagerness that could not be
> denied.
>
> Windows overran with them. Bud and blossom,
> green leaves, and trailing vines, were everywhere.
> The little yard was full, and the superintendent

proceeded to build a greenhouse, where, though he had never learned the art of floriculture, he had marvelous success. Soon a novel reward was suggested to the young vagabonds of Rivington Street,—and indeed of the whole region,—who flocked in, full of delight over the growing things.

One man's passion for plants transformed a community. People came from miles around to see the flowers. Children were encouraged to take plants home to grow on windowsills in whatever they had—tin cans or wooden boxes—until thousands of people had plants growing in their windows. The rampant enthusiasm for plants bred the first "Flower Mission of New York," which encouraged people to give flowers to the poor and to the sick children who were housed at the Sick Children's Mission. The initiative became so popular that a propagation area and greenhouse needed to be built. Its capacity increased to over 50,000 plants being propagated from seeds or cuttings, and the entire community needed to come together to help distribute over 100,000 bouquets and flowers to the sick and the poor. To this day, bringing flowers to someone in the hospital is common practice. It has its humble roots in one man's love for plants, which unexpectedly brought not only joy to people far and wide—but also united and uplifted a community of people around the simple act of growing and sharing plants with others.

You needn't be in a green-minded community to find the sense of well-being that plants provide. Matthew J. Wichrowski shared that in addition to horticultural therapy, which utilizes individual goals and treatment plans—often administered by a professional—there's also "therapeutic horticulture," which uses goals but is not measured or charted. In many cases, the stories that people have shared with me show personal explorations of everyday therapeutic horticulture.

> "My grandma tended to her garden as much as she could up until her death. She loved touching the soil with her bare hands. I find this direct contact therapeutic as well. Tending to my plants indoors and on my balcony is precious to me. I have struggled with chronic depression, chronic pain, and anxiety for a long time. When it was really bad, tending to my plants was the biggest responsibility I could handle; caring for pets would have been too much. I see my plants as pets, to be honest. They make me happy when they thrive. Their resilience gives me hope about overcoming bad stuff. They've also taught me that I can't control everything." —Tove T.

> "Last year, I learned that I have a heart condition that makes me very susceptible to heart attacks, and I had to have a defibrillator implanted. I spent a lot of time in my room to recover from the operation and to study, and I became quite depressed. But I had one nice hanging plant in my room. Eventually, I wanted more. I started collecting plants. Now my room is a jungle. Whenever I have to study

or if I have a lot of pain from my scars, I can really come to rest instead of becoming depressed in my little room."
—Simon

"I tend to isolate myself socially due to mental illness on top of my 'selective sound sensitivity,' also known as misophonia, which makes the presence of human beings (and the sounds their bodies make) extremely difficult for me to tolerate. Plants distract me from the human world just enough to help me better deal with it. The plant community on the internet motivates me to be more social. Whenever plants are the topic of a conversation, I light up a little. My desire to visit botanical gardens helped me to go out more, using public transportation for the first time by myself and building my confidence in traveling alone." —Franziska

"Living with major depression, there are many mornings when I find it difficult to leave my bed or even open the curtains to let the sun in—but my plants give me motivation to do just that. Because I know that they need the sunlight to thrive, I'm able to get out of bed, let the sun in, and relish in the energy it brings. The joy of seeing my plants thrive is immense. They are a reminder that life contains beauty and that I can have a hand in cultivating it, even when I'm feeling at my worst. That is absolutely priceless." —Hannah S.

"After years of therapy and misdiagnoses, I learned I have severe inattentive ADHD. . . . I have discovered that my morning and evening plant-care routines—remembering to water and prune my plants—help me to focus and set some intentions for the day. . . . Plants are my refuge from the noise my different brain produces. They wrap me in their energy like a blanket." —Pamela Garnett

As these and the other stories throughout this book show, plants clearly have the gift to heal and are integral to healthy environments and healthy people. But if this is the case, then as we have moved away from nature and into cities—seeking to reach our fullest potential—why have so many of us still failed to bring plants with us?

GET-GROWING EXERCISE: EVALUATION

1. How much time did you spend outdoors or with plants growing up? How much time do you spend now? What has caused that discrepancy, if any?

2. How can you bring more nature or elements of the outdoors into your life? Make a list of ideas.

3. In the coming weeks, try a few items on your list. As you bring more nature or elements of the outdoors into your life, how does it make you feel? Write down your impressions.

WE ONLY LOVE WHAT WE NOTICE

Let us twine our toes into roots, surge with the sap
and hearken to great trees. For theirs is a life that is older
than animalness, deeper than thought, and that may
well penetrate the primordial genesis of us all.

—Guy Murchie, The Seven Mysteries of Life

· · · · · · · · · · ·

*"When I watch plants grow, develop, and change, it satisfies my
curiosity. It's a wonder to behold the uniqueness of each plant, how
plants have different needs and respond differently to our touch.
I love running my hands over each leaf, thorn, and spine. I can
feel, see, touch, taste, smell—all of my senses are engaged. I have
learned to be patient, resourceful, smart, and observant thanks to
gardening. I do not see plants as just a patch of green on soil. I see
each individual plant, and each one is unique."* —Gem Yuson

L ike most city dwellers, you may not know where to start when it comes to communing with nature yet may be eager to receive some of the healing benefits we just covered. You may also be thinking: *where I live, there simply is no nature to enjoy.* This is not true—and I'll show you why. Luckily, enjoying nature wherever you live can be as simple as shifting your perspective. In this chapter, we'll explore how.

There is plenty of evidence that city people have begun to lose touch with nature. No shame, no blame—it's just what happens when something or someone isn't consistently part of our lives. We drift away from healthy habits and forget how good a workout or a session on the yoga mat feels. Inseparable childhood or school friends fall out of touch after growing up and graduations. Even spouses drift apart if enough time goes by without meaningful interaction. It's no different with our relationship with nature.

"Nature-deficit disorder," a description coined by journalist Richard Louv, may not be an accepted medical diagnosis today, but it's a useful term for summarizing the harm done to human health and well-being when one becomes distant or even alienated from the natural world. Several studies have shown that this decline in time outdoors—the disconnection from farm, field, and forest—is likely responsible for another popularized nonmedical term, "plant blindness," coined in 1998 by botanists James Wandersee and Elisabeth Schussler, which refers to "the inability to see or notice the plants in one's own environment."

Frank Dugan, a research plant pathologist at the United States Department of Agriculture, conducted a study in modern-day London on plant blindness and overall botanical literacy. He found that students, graduates, and a substantial portion of biology teachers could scarcely recognize ten common wildflowers. Yet eight of the ten of the wildflowers were referred to in Shakespeare, and all appear in British folklore—evidence that they were once common knowledge to most people, educated and not. The relatively rapid loss of knowledge and even recognition of plants, Frank believes, is not necessarily a result of our tendency to have a greater affiliation with animals than with plants (a viewpoint known as *zoocentrism*), but an indicator that we've started to lose connection to our natural world by not being in it.

Does this mean we need to take day trips to the countryside? Hike some trails? Go apple-picking? All of that is great to do, but the good news is that communing with nature—and thus reaping its benefits—is less about *seeking* and more about simply *seeing*. To do that, you may need to not only adopt a more leisurely pace but also afford yourself some spaciousness of mind to give yourself the opportunity to observe and delight in the most mundane of nature's artifacts. How? Well, by noticing plants, observing them, and getting curious about what life looks like from where they sit. When you do, you may begin to discover a world of wonder right outside your door.

I was recently brought in to help a client brainstorm business models that would encourage more people to garden. "Plant blindness is real," my client asserted when I mentioned the term. He pointed to the fact that one of my colleagues—the person who brought me into the job in the first place—hadn't noticed the copious number of plants in the client's offices when they first met, likely only registering them as part of the office backdrop.

Plant blindness has more far-reaching effects than inhibiting someone from walking into a plant store. As you can imagine, if you don't even recognize plants, it can lead to a failure to see their importance in our lives as well as their significance in the greater biosphere, or living system of our Earth. This in turn leads to less attention to and funding in the world of conservation and policy, for example. In the United States, 57 percent of the federally endangered species are in fact plants—but less than 4 percent of money spent on threatened and endangered species is used to protect them.

This disparity is striking when one considers that plants largely serve as the foundation for healthy ecological systems. Worldwide, 2,550 locations have been identified as Important Plant Areas— regions of internationally significant populations of threatened plant species, threatened habitats, and/or areas that exhibit exceptional botanical richness. But these areas receive only limited protection in some cases and come under numerous threats ranging from construction to agriculture to climatic shifts. You can see how it becomes a dangerous feedback loop: less attention on plants means less conservation of plants, less space for plants, and even fewer opportunities for our own interaction with plants, particularly in their native habitats.

Getting back to our analogy of losing touch with relationships in our lives: If you don't connect with someone, how can you have a relationship with them? And if you don't have that relationship, how will you experience its positive, life-affirming benefits? It is no different with our relationship with plants.

Luckily for us, plant blindness is curable, as my work and the work of others has shown. In a recent study known as "The Pet Plant Project," over 200 students were asked to grow an unknown plant from seed, monitor its development, and interact with their plant on a daily basis. Though no control group was present in this study, the researchers qualitatively found that the majority of students noticed plants more after the project and planned to grow plants in the future. Similarly, after my brainstorming session with the client, many of my colleagues professed a newfound love and appreciation for plants. Some approached me afterward to inquire about plant care. This also often happens at my plant workshops—people approach me wanting to know more, particularly after discovering some of the inner mysteries that plants have to offer. Turns out once you get even a basic understanding of plants, the joy and inspiration of having them in your life can be contagious!

> "When I was in dental school, it was really stressful. I
> decided to get a rose plant, an aloe plant, and a money plant
> to keep in my student hostel. They gave me the best
> moments in the hostel. I was ecstatic to see my new rose
> blooms [and] my money plant growing so quickly and
> [to use] the aloe in home remedies. When I was leaving the

hostel, a junior student asked me if she could take care of my plants. I was happy to pass on a legacy."
—Sreeja Renju Nair

"After my father-in-law died, I was overcome by grief. My blood-test results also showed I was deficient in vitamin D. Although it was pure coincidence, being in the sun to increase my vitamin D levels reminded of me of how much I missed my father-in-law. I would often ask him about his plants. He loved camellias, and they produced blooms the size of my hand. I started to plant camellias. I was outdoors every day, getting my free vitamin fix. Soon I ventured into planting geraniums, azaleas, roses, and more. I LOVE IT!!! And to my surprise, my plants are now enjoyed by my husband and children. It's wonderful when my children play the piano and the clarinet among the greenery. It's a beautiful music jungle for all to enjoy." —L. Mak

"When my daughter was seventeen, she and I never saw eye to eye. One day, after one of her awful, episodic screaming fits, I blurted out that she was a 'mean bitch.' I think we both looked shocked because I just couldn't believe I said that. She stormed out of the house. A bit later, I left to get dinner from the grocery store. I always stop in the floral section when I'm there. That day, the first plant I saw was a red, heart-shaped *Anthurium*. I stood there and had a little cry. Then I got what I needed for dinner—and went back and bought that plant. When I got home, I wrote a long, heartfelt letter to my daughter and gave it to her with the plant. We worked things out. Fast-forward to her college graduation five-plus years later. I'm glad to say that we'd grown closer during that time. While I was helping her move out of the dorm, she asked me to get her 'bitch plant' from the window! I had no idea what she was talking about. She explained that it was the plant I'd given her after calling her a 'bitch' years earlier. She said that the plant reminded her of how I never gave up on her and loved her even during the hard days. She said that when things got tough, she'd talk to the plant as if she were talking to me. Now when I see that plant, I feel a pang of guilt, but I also feel happy that it gave me an opportunity to reconnect with my daughter.

In addition to plants bringing my daughter and me closer, I remember my mother and grandmother used to grab snippets of plants to root in water and then pot. Each plant told a story. One was from a funeral, another from a wedding, another from a vacation. I have continued this tradition—for example, [with] rooting clippings from the plants at my daughter's wedding. These plants give me feelings of peace and closeness with my loved ones and friends. My husband participates, too: he gave me an orchid before he deployed to Iraq. I nursed and protected it and wanted it to be there when he came home. It meant the world to me that it bloomed again while he was gone and the blooms seemed to last forever. I felt as if it knew how much my soul needed to see it in bloom. It's now been in our family since 2005, and my husband and I both cherish this sweet orchid that still blooms." —Deanna Lynn Cole

Whether you're a seasoned plant carer or just starting out, a great way to get in tune with growing things is to engage in what I call "active observation" of plants. This can not only sharpen your plant-care skills but also calm your mind by slowing the pace of life and helping you savor the moment. Peaceful interludes can be carved out in even the most bustling cityscape. Plants can be your ally in this uplifting odyssey. All you need to do is make the conscious decision to notice nature.

I set that intention each morning when I go for a walk. One plant I always pass on these walks is a persistent smooth sumac (*Rhus glabra*) with pinnately compound leaves that spread like large green plumes on bright red leaf stems. I consider her persistent because she has established herself in a most insignificant crack in the concrete sidewalk, which abuts a brick wall. Somehow, the shrubby *Rhus*, which grows outward from the wall at a forty-five-degree angle, has prospered for years in this seemingly inhospitable space, reaching nearly seven feet (2.1 meters) over the course of the last growing season. How she found and conquered the crack to begin with may have been by luck or by pluck—or more likely, a little bit of both. Given her position, I imagine a mourning dove—or some other feathered wildfowl—feasting on her red berries in winter and relieving itself off the side of the building, fertilizing the *Rhus* on the way out. Often, seeds of plants pass unharmed through the digestive system of birds or beasts, ensuring not only that the seed will be transported away from its original mother plant but also that it will have a rich, fertile medium—in this case, bird poop—to grow in.

I often wonder if and how the sumac, a colony-forming species, spreading by root suckers, will solve for her solitude. If left unperturbed, it may take many years for this narrative to play out. Perhaps her serpentine, subterranean roots will slowly widen the crevice, inviting new growth. Or perhaps she will have to wait for Old Man Winter to thrust his icy fingers below the concrete to expand and tear back the coarse, gray girdle containing her. Or she may remain forever single, a true wallflower in every sense of the word, sealed to her fate by the happenstance of her home. (Unlike us humans, plants can't pull up roots and move if they don't like the climate, the real estate, or the social scene. They must grow where they're planted—do or die—and rely on seed or spore for their lineage to travel.) Or there may be outside intervention—say, a new development that goes up in her space. Then she may be unceremoniously uprooted, and my daily observation and relationship with this fellow urban citizen will come to an end.

Observations such as these allow us to be present and have a change of pace, even if the pace around us has not altered. They also allow us to appreciate change over longer periods of time—in this case, a plant's sense of time. Daily changes, like that of my neighborhood *Rhus*, may be virtually imperceptible or infinitesimal at best, but over the course of a season, or several years, the changes can be quite noticeable and impressive—that is, if we take the time to notice.

These practices in observation, particularly if done on a daily basis, set us up to more easily have profound experiences and interactions with nature—not just in the city, but anywhere we encounter her. Building upon our daily observations and playing out possible scenarios, as I did with my *Rhus*, can give us a sense of fellowship, neighborliness, and even civic duty toward our chlorophyllic compatriots. I experienced this on another one of my morning strolls—in the opposite direction of the *Rhus*—involving an abandoned *Bryophyllum delagoense*.

Now, *Bryophyllum delagoense* is otherwise known as a maternity plant or mother of thousands plant. That in itself tells you something about the strength of its life force. This plant is a succulent native to Madagascar and thus accustomed to drought and severe neglect. In sum, this Brooklyn bryo was a born survivor.

The neighborhood I was walking in was largely under construction, and a home-goods store had closed, leaving behind a precariously large and tangled plant, peering out of one of its sunny windows. I stopped, stepped closer, and returned her gaze. The fleshy succulent, nearly as tall as I am, stood in a planter on the floor, leaning her heft on the glass. We were separated by just a thin pane, yet there was no way for me to get into the building, so I walked on. But I kept an eye on her.

One day, months later, I saw a worker in the building. Tools, dust, and wood scraps were strewn everywhere, yet the long-suffering maternity plant, still surviving in its dusty planter, stood steadfast and stoic. I asked if I could take the plant off his hands.

"Come back tomorrow," the gruff worker told me. "My foreman will be in and you can ask him."

I followed up the next morning, garden shears in hand, and asked the foreman my question. "Do what you want with it," he replied, waving his hand.

There was no way I could carry this enormous plant home. So I snipped a selection of aging stems, placed the gnarled cuttings in a giant bag, and took them home. There, I laid them out in a row on my hardwood floor. I counted no less than fifteen stems from my rescue plant and a prolific number of plantlets—clonal plants that form along the leaf margins of the mother plant and propagate on the ready (hence the name "maternity plant" or "mother of thousands"). I repotted them all in a giant planter a few days later, after the cuts had calloused over so the stems wouldn't rot, and gave my newfound plant some southern exposure. She sits with me now as I write her story, happily making babies and coexisting with the other houseplants in my bedroom.

Rescuing plants is monumentally rewarding. Even in a small space, you can decide to take in a few plants in need. Find one that someone who's moving has set out by the curb (I took in two orphaned plants this way recently). Scroll through sites like Craigslist, which always seems to have some freebies for those who are thrifty. "Dumpster dive" outside big-box stores, which seem to cast off their all-too-often neglected plants. Buy one of those straggling money trees crowded on a shelf near the checkout at your local grocery, shivering in cold drafts as the doors open and close. Stow away a plantlet from the anemic spider plant that's been languishing on the file cabinet at work, put it in some loose soil in an old jam jar on your windowsill to see it root, then plant it lovingly in a hanging pot, and in a few months you'll be enjoying your morning coffee or tea while sun streams through its punky foliage. In return for modest doses of attention and patience, plants will literally stand by you through thick and thin.

> "A few years back I hit a little rough patch in life and I
> decided to pay a visit to my local plant shop. I didn't buy
> anything that day but I couldn't stop thinking about getting

a plant for my home. The next day I returned to the store and bought two plants—a deep red *Philodendron* and a pretty *Hoya*. I would wake up every morning and tend to my plants. Pretty soon I started to notice new growth and that really helped re-center me and remind me to see the good in the world." — Julia K.

"I realized last fall that I had seasonal depression. I needed something to help me smile and be productive. So I bought some succulents . . . which soon spiraled into growing from seed and leaf propagating. Over that winter I received rescue houseplants from my job and my grandmother. I started to learn how to rehab neglected plants. I even accidentally put my newly bought *Maranta* and moon valley *Pilea* into shock, but over the months brought them back. In doing so, I kind of brought myself back. There is something so therapeutic about making things grow and helping plants thrive." —Cole A.

I also see volunteering at my local community garden four hours a week during the growing season as a moving meditation that can elevate mind, heart, and energy. I visited so often that I eventually inquired about becoming a member. The garden—a quarter-acre plot—is sizable by city standards and is a hidden gem for many people, particularly those who have been in the community for decades. With every branch pruned, every shovelful of soil turned, every flower planted—each action is like needlepoint, threading you tighter into the tapestry of the community that you call home.

"I'm a board member at [my local] botanical community garden. I joined when I was going through a rough time, and found getting my hands in the soil and caring for plants instantly elevated my mood. The garden also proved to be fertile ground for new friendships. I made several close friends. We bonded over our shared love of nature and plants." —Christina Cobb

"After a traumatic incident, I found peace in plant-time. There is a slow and quiet delight in watching incremental change and being more attuned to the seasons. My growing love of plants caused me to join a plant society—my first steps back into a social world. I ended up applying for and getting into a horticultural course, which has been world changing. Plants are a constant source of wonder in what can be a disheartening world. It is among plants that I find hope, peace of mind, and a quiet heart." —Tessa Kum

Admittedly, it may require some time to take notice of plants. You may need to be a bit more deliberate in your observations, as I had been with the *Rhus*. Plants, after all, are nuanced in their charm, subtle in affect. Theirs is a fleeting glance across a crowded dance floor, a clandestine rendezvous between two lovers under the dark hood of night, a momentary breath of wind on a hot, still day. For most of us, plants seem to be completely immobile, unresponsive, and just a pixelated blur of green. However, as we'll explore in the chapters to come, plants are anything but unmoving—and offer a variety of dazzling colors, shapes, forms, and mysteries that they generously share.

GET-GROWING EXERCISE: OBSERVATION

1. **Pick a plant to observe on one of your walks around your neighborhood** over the course of a week, two weeks, a month, or even an entire season. It could be something as insignificant as a dandelion (*Taraxacum officinale*) in a crack of a sidewalk, a coleus (*Plectranthus scutellarioides*) in a window box, or a giant oak tree (*Quercus* sp.) in a neighbor's backyard. Make mental notes as to how that single plant looks each day. What color are the leaves? Is the plant pointing in a particular direction? Is it in flower? Is it leafier on one side?

2. **Craft possible explanations around your observations.** Once you make your plant observations, begin creating stories that might explain why something is the way it is. For instance, is the leafier side of the oak tree due to the amount of sun it's getting in the afternoon? Or is it because someone cut the tree on one side to prevent it from hitting a telephone wire?

3. **Note one subtle change and one major change over time.** Did the leaves orient themselves differently over the course of a day? Did acorns start to form on the oak tree? The benefit to looking for both subtle and major shifts will hone your ability to detect changes over time. With practice, you'll find yourself making mental notes about the pace "your" plant is operating at—which is more than likely different from your pace!

WHEN A TREE FALLS
IN THE FOREST . . .

We abuse land because we see it as a commodity belonging
to us. When we see land as a community to which we belong,
we may begin to use it with love and respect.

—Aldo Leopold

. . . .

*"Plants remind me that we're all interconnected and that my life
comes from a long line extending all the way back to the beginning
of life's existence—and if my predecessors delivered me to this
point in time, I, too, will be fine." —Eric @aroiddaddy*

One of my first lessons in how we can affect our environment—and how it in turn affects us—came when I was a teenager working to restore a coal-mine site near my hometown. I was tasked with helping to try to put the pieces of this landscape back together in order to get plants to grow again and restore the ecosystem's health. The largest and most eye-opening part of the job was designing the planting plan for the restoration of Grassy Island Creek, one of the many brownfields[1] that had been laid to waste by the coal-mining industry—an all-too-common scene in my hometown.

Attempting to restore a mine site is no easy feat. The land had little growing on it—save for the occasional sickly looking, gray birch (*Betula populifolia*) poking through the craggy substrate. There were a few dense thickets of invasive Japanese knotweed (*Fallopia japonica*), whose cane-like stems and quick growth have earned it the name "Japanese bamboo." Other than that, the land was in ruin—a heap of black rock that looked as if it had been

---

1 A brownfield is a former industrial or commercial site where future use is affected by real or perceived environmental contamination.

dropped on the planet in molten form and then congealed and cooled.

I found myself on a mine site where my great-grandfather could have very well worked when he was around my age, looking to "undo" what he or other men like him were tasked to do. A trail of vapor, like the hot breath of a sleeping dragon, rose up out of a mine shaft, which appeared like a black, crusted wound on the earth's surface.

After felling much of Pennsylvania's original forests, anthracite coal mining began to alter the landscape. My great-grandfather worked in the mines picking coal for over fifteen years, starting at the tender age of eighteen. I wasn't inquisitive enough as a child to ask him about his work, so my grandmother now serves as the conveyor of much of his past. As his health waned in his old age, she asked her father to write down everywhere he had worked as a young man, so as not to lose a piece of his history.

I found it there on writing paper, which my grandmother had neatly tucked away in her Bible nearly twenty years prior. Slowly, I worked out his labored penmanship. His statements were plain and pointed, unembellished and uncomplaining—all qualities that my great-grandfather possessed when he was alive: "First started in Dickson to work in mines. After five years there, then to Miles Slope, Olyphant. Then to Rogers Coal Mine in Scranton. Then to Eddy Creek for the Hudson Coal Company in Olyphant; and then Swader Mine."

Though my great-grandfather had never complained, my grandmother shared that his labor was unforgiving. He would trudge home from the mines in the winter months, wet with sweat and snow. By the time he arrived, his clothes were stiff from the ice that clung to the fabric. A few years after he married my great-grandmother, the cost of ceaseless extraction of coal had imprinted on his lungs as much as it had on the land and air, a testament that the Earth—and we—may have been better off had the coal been left underground.

Coal mining isn't as extant now in the northeastern counties, where I'm from, largely due to a 1959 disaster at the Knox Mine in Exeter and Pittston, where the Susquehanna River broke through the cavernous mine, killing twelve men. Coal cars were shuttled to the mouth of the gaping hole to try to plug up what had become an underground waterfall. To think that we had dug enough tunnels underneath the Earth's surface to make millions of gallons of river disappear! Well, that's black magic if there ever was such a thing. Though coal use was already waning by 1959—having earlier been fueled by the overharvesting of wood, the wars, and the railroads—the Knox Mine Disaster put the final nail in the coffin for deep mining.

Humans are the ultimate procrastinators. Just like waiting until we have a health scare to change our diet or adopt a fitness routine, or leaving a stress-filled job only after we have a nervous break-down, we seem to wait until disaster strikes before we reach the re-alization that we need to stop or at least alter our original plans. Now, hydraulic fracturing, or "fracking," the 380-million-year-old natural-gas seams in the Marcellus Shale thousands of feet beneath the earth has taken precedence over the pursuit of coal.[2] Hydraulic fracturing involves breaking fissures in the earth and using water

---

2 The Marcellus Shale is a formation of marine sedimentary rock, plankton, and other materials that was deposited during the Devonian period and is now commonly extracted for natural gas.

and poisonous chemicals at high pressure to extract oil or gas—the ancient remains of plants and other organic matter.

Exploring the site at Grassy Island Creek, I bent down under the heat of the sun and picked up some ashen rock. One of the first things we would need to do would be to create a substrate for roots to grow. Soil would need to be brought in—a lot of it. We'd also need to heavily lime the area to neutralize the highly acidic substrate. Most plants—or other life-forms—can't live in such harsh environments.

Lastly, the land and river would need to be restored to a more natural shape to give the restoration a chance (to optimize access to the coal, the river had been *channelized*: siphoned through large cement troughs that gravely restricted its natural flow).

A fluvial geomorphologist was brought in to "redesign" the river, sculpting and shaping its path like a surgeon of landscapes, restoring it to anatomical correctness. He added riffles and runs, reintroducing spaces for algae, aquatic insects, and ultimately future fish. Once the soil and plants were in place, the rest of the habitat would, theoretically, take care of itself.

A planting plan came next. It was my job to decide what trees would be best suited for the compromised terrain, how many to start with, and where and at what distances they should be planted. I naturally chose native trees, with the exception of a cultivar of shrub willow, which was explicitly bred for planting on marginal lands such as mine sites. I looked for a combination of species, including fruiting varieties like serviceberry (*Amelanchier* sp.), eastern redbud (*Cercis canadensis*), and dogwood (*Cornus* sp.) to attract wildlife and nitrogen-fixers such as alders (*Alnus* sp.) and locusts (*Robinia* sp.), which can help rebuild soil. I also chose some ash

(*Fraxinus* sp.), oaks (*Quercus* sp.), and maples (*Acer* sp.) to add a more native mix of plants, as it can be very easy for one prolific species, like locusts, or invasive species, like Japanese knotweed, to take hold before others can establish themselves.

The area was seeded, largely with birdsfoot trefoil (*Lotus corniculatus*) inoculated with a nitrogen-fixing bacteria, *Rhizobium lupini* (the trefoil is a commonly found drought-resistant branching legume with a beautiful canary-yellow crown of flowers); nitrogen-fixing white clover (*Trifolium repens*); and a mixture of some slow-growing grass species. This would help bring more life to the soil by adding fertility, slowing erosion, and providing some coverage and better conditions for seedling survival.

The 1.5-acre (.6 hectare) area of Grassy Island Creek seemed to transform over the course of weeks. But our success was short-lived. When a windstorm ravaged the area a year later, there were no older forests, microorganisms, roots, soil, and groundcover to offer a natural windbreak and built-in erosion and flood control. Only the areas that had been left mostly untouched by mining survived.

It takes a lot longer to repair environmental destruction than it does to perpetuate it. Despite our best intentions, our best efforts, and a good supply of resources, we couldn't repair even a small sliver of ecosystem that Mother Nature had methodically laid down and evolved over hundreds of millions of years before—a miracle of millennia that we had undone in a mere six or seven generations.

From this experience, I learned that one thing is for certain: there will never be a better mother for nature than Mother Nature herself. Perhaps, then, before we remove, extract, or destroy, we must ask ourselves: Are we prepared to step in and be the surrogate of this landscape for an unforeseeable number of years afterward?

Should we continue to appropriate the millennia of compressed plants below the surface, burn them so determinedly that the rain turns acidic from the fumes, and then dump the unused remainder on the land, left in such ravaged condition that nothing will grow for centuries thereafter? Or can we learn from our doings and instead ask: as beings who are part of nature, how can we learn from her?

We don't have to make nature sick—nor, as happened to my great-grandfather and so many others, people sick as well. Through selective culling, we can make forest systems healthier. And with good planning and involvement, we can make our communities more livable and healthier. We can make our homes more calming and inviting. All we need to do is turn to nature—listen to her, observe her ways, and emulate her to the best of our ability. There's much for us to gain by doing so.

Plant blindness, which we discussed in the previous chapter, points to a larger issue holding us back from experiencing all the benefits of nature. Nature often is unnoticed, unappreciated, and abused because, by and large, we—especially those of us who live in cities—have been infected by a commodity mind-set. Nature has become an object of consumer culture, masked and marketed with little resemblance to its original state. This chapter will ask you to push your mind beyond the constraints of modern consumerism and start recognizing how beholden we are to nature's (dwindling) bounty, and how much more ubiquitous plants are in our lives than we may realize, far beyond the potted bromeliads and the poinsettias we purchase over the winter—even to the point of inhabiting our language. In this chapter, I'll dare you to see the world from a plant's perspective.

Plant perspective: Nature is more than "resources"

A decade before my sojourn to British Columbia's Great Bear Rainforest, the area was unceremoniously known as the "Mid-Coast Timber Supply Area." This expanse of land, most of which is only accessible by boat, was the frontline for industrial logging in Canada—a place where wood was cut to be pulped for paper products like books and magazines, perhaps like the one you're reading now.[3] Given its original name, the public may have only ever had the impression that this wide expanse of wilderness was a logging zone.

I had a rare opportunity to travel to Great Bear as part of an excursion to assist in raising awareness and funds for the area. A group of local and international conservation organizations and the First Nations indigenous people had banded together to conserve the Canadian region. At the time of our journey, it was announced that the first 7 million acres (2.8 million hectares) of old-growth forest would be under strict protection, with a five-year plan to incorporate conservation and human well-being throughout the region. Great Bear today now spans 15 million acres (6.1 million hectares) under various forms of conservation, management, and protection, from the northern tip of Vancouver Island to the Alaska border, and is part of the largest expanse of coastal temperate rain forest in the world. Big? Yes. But it's still considered rare, since temperate rain forests cover less than 1 percent of the Earth's land mass.

---

3 This book is made with 30 percent post-consumer recycled paper.

Given that much of this area is on the Pacific coast, and in some cases dotted across myriad islands, fourteen of us would be living on a boat for two weeks to get a good feel for the place. We departed from Bella Bella, a picturesque seaside town on Campbell Island in British Columbia and home of the Heiltsuk First Nation, heading north toward Princess Royal Island.

The bow of our boat parted the cool, steely waters of the narrowing bay. A thin film of rain, which seemed ever present, kissed our skin. The atmosphere cradled so much moisture in its airy bassinet that it gave the effect of looking at the world through frosted glass. Around us, craggy cliffs rose to such great heights that some were obscured beneath a dense tulle of fog. The fog likely formed at sea, condensing over the cool water and land as it moved through the air. It meandered for miles above the bay, grazing the rock faces like a flock of ethereal sheep. The trees, a mixture of red cedar (*Thuja plicata*) and Sitka spruce (*Picea sitchensis*)—some up to a thousand years old—clung to the escarpments, standing shoulder to shoulder like sentinels, soaring skyward against a stone backdrop.

Our captain spotted a group of waterfalls to the port side. We could hear the dull roar of the cataracts over the motor. The captain inched the boat just close enough for us to feel the icy spume on our faces. Standing at the stern, we could feel the great rumble of the water reverberate through our bodies, our screams of delight drowned out by its sheer, thunderous force. I've lived much of my life in nature and seen countless heart-stopping vistas. But never had I felt so dwarfed, so humbled, so overawed by a landscape.

One stop on our trip took us to a well-hidden sandy shore. Our cultural guide from the Kitasoo First Nation, Doug Neasloss, a well-built, handsome man with a chiseled face and crew cut, kindly asked us to remove our hats. The area where he was taking us was a sacred space—little known to outsiders. We trekked into the forest until we approached two hefty trees, each at least four feet (1.2 meters) in diameter and about a hundred feet (30.5 meters) in length, both of which had been felled to create horizontal beams. They were parallel and spaced a good distance from one another, elevated from the forest floor atop four more equally robust tree-beams, at least ten feet (3 meters) high. As we approached, we could see that they floated above a sunken area, shaped like a square hollowed out in the forest floor. The "stage," which had now been overtaken by ferns of all kinds, was flanked on all four sides by long bleacher-like steps, making the whole area look like a mossy amphitheater. I could imagine the area as a mystical performance stage for the dryads and sylphs of the forest.

For millennia, this space was used to host *potlatches*—sacred, communal ceremonies that drew multiple First Nations peoples together in solidarity. Our guide told us that potlatches would be hosted here clandestinely even when the Canadian government banned the ceremonies from 1884 to 1951—a tactic to assimilate the native peoples and crush their culture. Now we stood in this forest space, which for Douglas and his people was considered not only a sacred space and home but also a symbolic place of resistance.

On our way back to the boat, we took pause to rest our legs on a pile of felled trees that were several hundred years old. Some were long enough to sit seventy or more people, side by side. I removed my shoes and wet socks and let my shriveled toes feel the first sunlight we'd had in days. The faint smell of salt and seaweed from the lapping water rose on the air. Ross McMillan, the president of Tides Canada and one of the architects of the Great Bear Rainforest project, shared that the trees we were resting on had been illegally cut down by loggers. Given the sensitive and sacred nature of the area, swift action was taken to stop further encroachment. What may have looked like good wood for export for a lumber company was part of a rare, intact ecosystem and a sacred space to the people who lived there.

"I recently visited an area where loggers were felling trees just like this," another of our boatmates mused. "Japanese script had been spray-painted in red on the side of one of the logs."

Curious as to where these trees would end up, he had approached one of the lumberjacks to inquire if he knew.

"Yeah. They're en route to Japan!" the lumberman yelled over the scream of the saw. "To be turned into chopsticks."

Sitting on this majestic fallen tree, in this magical place, after hours of travel on fog-shrouded waters, past earth-shaking waterfalls and towering cliffs, I shuddered at the thought that this entire landscape could have been converted to something as insignificant as disposable chopsticks. These trees are not disposable. Nature recycles and uses every bit of her creations—rooted or not. We, as a society, on the other hand, over centuries of migration away from close interaction with nature, have lost touch with our ability to see the continuous cycle of nature and how our products and actions affect, interrupt, and can irrevocably destroy processes and potentials that have endured for millennia. When we continuously and mindlessly assault nature, we reduce our chances, opportunities, and motivation to save spaces such as these.

How can we break that negative cycle? When we create the interest, space, or time to commune with nature on a deeper level rather than heedlessly using what she produces, we reconnect to our environment and that which we receive from her. The more we practice, the deeper our relationship with nature becomes.

IN THE 1700S, George Berkeley, an Anglican bishop and philosopher, presented a theory known as "immaterialism," which essentially boiled down to his belief that there are no real material objects, only our perception of them. Through the ages, his queries evolved (or became synthesized) into a single, provocative query that is commonly heard today: "If a tree falls in a forest and no one is around to hear it, does it make a sound?"

I'd like to pose an even deeper metaphysical question: "If a tree falls in the forest, is it still a tree?" Does a tree relinquish its "treeness" as soon as it's severed from its roots? Is it still a tree once it has been fully feasted on by wood-boring insects and tissue-eating fungi until only its soiled traces remain? To help us think about this question, we should consider that a tree that has been struck down by lightning, cracked in half, or cut off at the base by a saw can sometimes sprout new life. It is more often than not aided in this process by its brothers and sisters and mycorrhizal and microbial networks, shuttling nutrients through its intact root system, thereby safeguarding not only its life but the overall integrity of the ecosystem. Sometimes it starts as just a modest sprout or branch, but in time, there may be a new tree in its place.

There are plenty of examples of trees and plants that spring forth new life from a single branch or even just a leaf. Willows (*Salix* sp.), like the ones near my grandmother's house, come to mind. After years of cutting and removal, they always seem to find a way to persist out of just a single branch left behind. Those of us with houseplants know which ones root more easily than others. Certain succulents, like *Sedum*, x *Graptosedum*, and *Graptopetalum*, need only a leaf, sheared cleanly off the stem base, to produce a new plant. And many *Kalanchoe* and *Bryophyllum* take it one step further by forming copious clonal plantlets along their leaf margins, which fall off like mini plant paratroopers, equipped with everything they need to survive, provided they find the right soil medium to subsist in—which, as anyone who grows them discovers, could be just about anything.

But suppose our felled tree decomposes rather than putting forth shoots of life. Is it now dead, no longer a tree? If its seeds were intact on the canopy when it was cut down—say, for example, it was an oak sporting its acorns—each acorn would have all the information to produce a whole new tree. It would only take one . . . and a new tree would be born of the old. Given time and proper conditions, multiple acorns could produce a veritable forest of their own kind—all from that one "dead" tree.

This leads to the question: When do trees cease being trees? Does a tree lose its "treeness" as soon as we insert the saw? Or is it when its noble wood gets converted to chopsticks—to be used momentarily over one's lunch and then carelessly discarded? Who are we to say a tree is no longer a tree?

In order to really understand the life of a living being—the full scope of its existence—we need to consider its life after "death"—and our role in that process. Once we connect our products and actions back, all the way back, to their origins in nature, we see that we are living far more closely with nature than we might expect. In a sense, we begin to hear that tree falling in the forest thousands of miles away. We begin to realize that nature is giving and giving to us every day. What are we giving back to nature?

Take a good look around you. The wooden beams, floorboards, tables, chairs, picture frames, trellises, bookshelves, jewelry boxes, and doors we pass through were all once trees with roots that clawed their way through soil and stone and raised their branches and leaves dutifully toward the sun. The cotton sheets that cover us at night were probably the result of an international web of businesses built upon plants: fluffy bolls picked, carded, combed, spun, woven, and designed in the United States, China, India, or any of over a dozen other countries all over the world. Even our polyester shirts were derived from storehouses of ancient algae locked beneath the earth's surface, as is most of the fuel that powers our vehicles and warms our homes. Rubber for everything from insulation to tires comes from trees originating in China, Thailand, Indonesia, and Vietnam. Our underwear could have been made from rayon, which is pulped from the forests of Canada, Europe, or Asia, for instance. The lotions, salves, balms, and oils that we use to clean and soften our skin have all originated in or been synthesized in some way from a plant's unique chemistry.

And there's more. The coffee that gets us moving in the morning, the tea that soothes us at night, and the wine or beer we imbibe to unwind—plants. The oils that make our candies, our soap, and what we sop up with our Italian bread at the restaurant have been pressed from everything from cottonseed to palm fruits to olives. The food we eat to nourish ourselves—from apples to farro, wild rice to zucchinis—or even the foods we eat not to nourish ourselves but to pleasure ourselves (*ahem*, high-fructose corn syrup) have their foundations in a plant-based existence. Even if you identify as the most ardent of meat eaters, you indirectly eat plants: Grass-fed or grain-fed? Pasture-raised or organically fed? You are what you eat, and whatever you eat eats.

This is more than a mere thought exercise. It's learning to reframe what we think of as "resources" as the body of nature herself. Take coal, for instance. Most of us no longer think of resources like coal as plants. Most of us were taught to consider such things in reduced, economic terms—as "fossil fuels" that power our vehicles and heat our homes. But coal is a plant that has simply morphed into a new form, swapping molecules for minerals, due to pressure and time. It is a life-form with a story to tell—individually and as a member of a larger community.

Is it not kind of strange, when you think about it, that we ravenously extract and burn millions-of-years-old decomposed life to power our clock, computer, or video-game console? Especially when every plant living here now and before us has worked out how to live off of solar power—the cleanest, most reliable form of energy on the planet? Perhaps they are not stymied by special interests and politics, but do we not have something to learn from them—and their millions of years of knowledge?

In another worldview, we might have considered fossilized plant remains as sacred objects. Instead of an energy resource, a 350-million-year-old nugget of anthracite coal—composed of the carbon-rich remains of plants and animals long since gone—could instead be considered an object fit for a museum. Similarly, fracking, in another way of thinking, would have been regarded as too invasive, too destructive, too unthinkable to effectuate.

Plants, in their native environments, take care of us, without needing us to care for them. They do this so adeptly, so invisibly, so graciously that their prodigious work is all but invisible—and that's something that we all too often take for granted. When you start appreciating plants beyond their aesthetic nature or their utility, enter their world, and seek to decode the eons of nature's "knowing" that they embody, you begin to appreciate a whole different perspective on plants—not just what they can do for us, but what they can teach us.

"I am a high school teacher. I created my own course on agriculture and gardening. I have seen a drastic change in my students' behavior and in myself. I love letting people know how beneficial and essential plants and nature are to being human." —John Sotiriadis

"Picking off my plants' dead leaves reminds me that every form of being has an ending, that death is truly a universal occurrence. That even though that hibiscus bloom only lasts for a day, it has fulfilled its purpose. The acceptance of losing a plant has helped me also accept the death of my best friend. It makes the cycle of life tangible." —Sarah Solange

"I appreciate all the birds and other wildlife my outdoor plants attract. It gives me a good feeling to know that my garden improves a space and makes it not only a space I enjoy but one that other animals enjoy, too." —Pia

Plant perspective: It's about integrity, not perfection

It might seem counterintuitive, but plants have more complex lives than we do in many ways. I talked about the "afterlife" of plants with Allan Schwarz, founder of the Mezimbite Forest Centre in Mozambique. "As humans, [when we die,] we just get burned, or buried—rotting away beneath the soil. Some of us have kids, which I suppose continues our DNA beyond our three score years and ten. But trees . . ." Allan pauses as if visualizing all the trees he has planted, salvaged, and felled over the years. "Some decompose—feeding the other wildlife left behind; some produce lots of seed to continue forward; and then others leave their long-lasting wood."

I visited Allan at his sustainable development organization outside of Beira in Mozambique. Trained as an architect and master craftsperson, Allan became a forest conservationist when he saw the trees in the forests he grew up with in South Africa being carelessly cut down and shipped overseas. "There is no reason why a land as rich as Mozambique," he once said, referring to its wealth in natural resources, "should be as poor as it is." He theorized that poverty was at the root of forest destruction, so he set out to help remedy that the way that he knew best—through working with wood.

Shortly after the country's civil war, he obtained a ninety-nine-year lease of land in the Sofala Province and set up a forest-conservation and woodworking shop, with the idea of training artisans not only to appreciate and work the wood but also to restore the forests and heal the land and heavy hearts.

"A product from the forest or field, whether it be oil from a coconut, seed from a sesame, or a board from a tree, still has resonance of the place from which it came," says Allan, "particularly if you respect the nature of its being and continue to be a good steward of the land."

Allan's products are representative of his care. His food products, which are largely sold to the local market, are produced with the highest integrity. Even oils, when pressed, are made with such care so as not to denature the enzymes, which in turn keeps the health benefits of the plants from which they are extracted intact for the people who use them. His wood products, turned or carved by hand, also are carefully conceived and designed to reveal the very nature of the tree from which they came and the events in its life. For example, if there is an inconsistency in the wood, like a crack or a hole, the wood is not discarded. It instead is repaired with a butterfly stitch, or a smaller piece of wood is meticulously cut to fit the hole. The wood's color, luster, hardness, weight, growth pattern, and grain—the latter as unique as a thumbprint—reveal the nature of the tree and even serve as a lens into its past life.

An example of observing how trees' growth patterns can reveal more of their stories. While hiking on the edge of one of the highest vertical cliffs in Thailand to accompany a local botanist in his documentation of rare plant species, I noticed how gnarled and twisted the trees were, like knotted, arthritic fingers poking through the blistered earth. Trees that spiral in their growth often indicate that they are growing, or have grown, at high elevations or on windy ridges, with this spiraling potentially helping to make the tree more flexible in weathering heavy winds and snow. Trees without definitive growth rings, like those from Mozambique, designate that they are from tropical areas, which don't have distinct seasons, whereas clear growth rings may indicate the tree grew in a climate with seasons, like the oaks and maples from my home state of Pennsylvania. Moreover, the growth rings reveal something about the tree's past. Broad, evenly spaced rings mean the tree enjoyed good weather; narrow rings reveal harder times—perhaps drought or even an insect infestation; and dark scarring could mean that the tree was bruised by fire or a lightning strike. Much like in a book of history or a journal, all of this information is recorded in the remains of the tree. When the wood of a tree is worked with the integrity of the tree in mind, the "story" of the tree is not lost, but rather can be integrated into the finished piece and enter into the life of whoever brings that piece into their home. This adds dimension and a closer relationship to plants in ways that are hard to quantify, but we know them when we feel them. In a similar way that eating dinner in your humble urban abode at the same scarred oak table Gram and Gramps had in their kitchen brings back the warmth and love of family and images of their faces around that table, so seeing the oak's well-worn wood and the inconsistencies in its grain brings you closer to that brave tree that grew alongside its siblings, weathering storms and wood-boring insects—and now quietly enhances your life in the heart of a bustling city.

The Japanese have an aesthetic philosophy known as *wabi-sabi*, which Allan's philosophy—something he refers to as "African Zen"—mirrors. It's essentially a view that accepts and embraces that beauty may very well be imperfect, impermanent, and incomplete. In this sense, idealized perfection does not exist. Instead of judging a piece of wood for its level of perfection—a board, say, with a fine grain and devoid of knots—a craftsperson practicing *wabi-sabi* would instead see beauty in every board, accepting that it may be warped, knotted, or pitted with holes. In turn, the crafts-person would then work with the inconsistencies, not only becoming a better, more skilled artisan—a true apprentice of the natural world—but also maintaining the nature and integrity of the wood. In a sense, the craftsperson works in harmony with the wood, teasing out the subtleties of its moods and, in turn, seeking to tell its truest story.

This might sound like a woo-woo idea that's more theoretical than real. But it's right there, in your relationship with any plant you've watered through a season or two:

> "My plants have taught me that life isn't perfect. Just like my plants, I can get sick, lose a leaf, or bend a little, but that doesn't make me less of a person. When I'm having a bad day, my plants remind me that it's OK. Because one dead leaf doesn't define a plant, and that goes for me, too."
> —Amy von Fisher

> "I've come to terms with the fact that the plants that I buy from the plant shop may not look the same as they continue to grow. Some get shaggy or leggy or bare. We can clip and prune them to help them along, but for the most part, they will change, as we all do." —Jocelyn C.

> "I received a bonsai from my mother's friend for my graduation and I really loved how it looked. It was by no means 'perfect,' but its structure, the way its branches curved to one side, made it that much more interesting. When I moved into my first apartment, I sat it on my

windowsill and often pondered about the plant and how it
grew the way it did." —Sully

"A car accident a few years ago left me with chronic pain, so
I spend quite a bit of time indoors now. Soon after [the
accident], I began collecting houseplants to give me a
positive activity to focus on. I really didn't know much
about plants, so I kind of just winged it, learning as I went.
Some plants, which I had far away from my windows, really
stretched and bent themselves toward the light. Another
actually started to cling to my wooden cabinet and became a
monster. The plants I have really showed to me their
persistence to be the best that they can be with the situation
they had been given, and that encouraged me to be more
proactive with my condition. Though I still have chronic
pain, I began doing yoga together with physical therapy, as
well as short walks to make my life better, too." —Libby

Plant perspective: Process, not product; beings, not things

Perhaps our view about plants has been restricted by the way we
have learned (or have not learned) to talk about them. Zen Bud-
dhists see language itself as one of the greatest limiters to deep understanding: *furyū monji* is a phrase that means "without dependence
on words or letters," denoting that the spoken word cannot ever
convey the full experience of reality.

I had never given much thought to how language might shape our experience of, feelings about, and perceptions of nature and our relationship to it—until my friend Randy Hayes, the founder of Rainforest Action Network, referred to *padapa*, the Sanskrit word for tree, which literally translates to "drinking at the foot" or "foot-drinking."

What comes to mind when you think of "foot-drinking"? You may imagine the living roots, connected to land, pulling up moisture, which travels up through the tree into the branches and leaves.

Randy elaborated on this idea: "A tree doesn't exist in isolation. When it does, it's because it's been cut off and is now called 'timber.' When it's a living tree, there's a nourishing nutrient and water cycle going up [through the roots to its leaves]. It drinks from the soil and [water] *evapotranspires* from the leaves that eventually forms the clouds, that drop the rain, [that] goes into the soil and comes back up [into the tree] again."

Randy's point: Would we be so keen to cut an animate being who drinks at the foot if we had a language that described a tree as such?

This was indeed a beautiful metaphor and a thought worth musing over. Larry McCrea, a professor at Cornell University who teaches Sanskrit, explained that in Sanskrit you can generate new words freely, provided that you use the basic building blocks of the language. Therefore, anyone could make up new words to describe a feeling, an object, or the world.

This fluid, poetic, "process-oriented" quality is not limited to Sanskrit. American Indian languages, like the Algonquian languages of Ojibwe and Potawatomi, are similarly supple, or polysynthetic. In a "polysynthetic language," as it was described to me by Autumn Mitchell, a native Ojibwe, smaller words can be strung together to form larger words. "In English we put sentences together with words," she explained. "But in polysynthetic languages, like Ojibwe, you do it at word level." This means a whole sentence can be one very long word, but that word will be resplendent with meaning: "'Apple pie,' as it's spoken in my language, might describe how the apple is grown, where it's from, and even who picked it."

Different languages also have different ratios of verbs, denoting processes, to nouns, denoting products or things. In her book *Braiding Sweetgrass*, botanist and Potawatomi Nation member Robin Wall Kimmerer shared that 70 percent of the Potawatomi language is composed of verbs, whereas the English language is only 30 percent verbs and is largely focused on nouns, which she sagely remarked seems apt in a culture highly focused on "things."

Autumn Mitchell confirmed that it's similar in Ojibwe: "Nouns are formed [by giving] a verb one of two endings. Endings for people or beings—and plants fall under 'beings'—have animate endings. Other items, like a bowl, would be inanimate. So instead of having a 'gendered' language, like you would see in maybe Spanish, you would have something differentiated as being alive or not alive. We [Ojibwe] identify many objects as animate that English speakers would deem inanimate."

Not all cultures view objects as inanimate, however. In the Japanese Shinto religion, certain inanimate objects, like a wooden bowl—particularly one made by a venerated craftsperson—may contain *kami*, which vaguely translates into "a spirit of nature." It's why the Japanese will traditionally decorate areas with *shimenawa*, a sacred rope, or install a *kamidana*, a miniature altar to enshrine *kami*, in their home. Certain trees, known as *yorishiro*, are said to attract and house spirits, and will often be tied with rope. Cutting down these trees would bring misfortune.

Considering how other people think and express themselves gave me a new perspective on how even the language we learned at our parents' knees can shape our relationship to the earth and the plants that inhabit it. Periodically, over my many years of immersion in nature, I've closed my eyes and tried to imagine what it would be like to be a tree. But now, inspired by these conversations, I wondered what would happen if I swapped in a different word: What would it be like to be a "foot drinker"?

Well, I mused, I would be both born of and married to the cool soil of the Earth, communicating silently and invisibly to my neighbors. My roots would not only speak to other roots of my own kind but would be able to translate and translocate between other organisms like bacteria and fungi. My leaves and my bark would perhaps do the same with insects, either drawing them near or warding them off. I would communicate with the sky, supplying it with both oxygen and water vapor, so that I—and the rest of the foot drinkers around me—could have a constant source of moisture via the sky, through cloud cover and precipitation, to preserve my long-lived existence so that I could mature, provide some seeds to the forest floor in the chance that they might propagate, and then slowly, silently, shed bark and branch until my body again found its way to the earth, my origins, but this time as *adamah* and *hava* ("living soil" in Hebrew), a gift not just for mankind—but for all kinds.[4]

---

4 The story of Adam and Eve is derived from the Hebrew words *adamah*, meaning "red clay" or "soil," and *hava*, meaning "living." In sum, they were born out of the "living earth."

SO NOW, TAKE PAUSE. HOW MANY PLANTS ARE AROUND
YOU AT THIS VERY MOMENT? DID YOUR NUMBER
INCREASE FROM WHEN YOU FIRST COUNTED?

GET-GROWING EXERCISE: ASSOCIATION

1. **Pick a plant-based object from your home**—it could be
   a coffee table, your favorite shirt, or a container of tea
   from your aunt, for instance. You may not know anything about its origins, but take a moment to think about
   what the plant's life may have been like before it took the
   form it now has. The product label may tell you where
   this plant became the table where you have breakfast,
   the shirt you shrug on in the morning, and the tea you
   sip. If you know the wood your table is made of, or the
   plant that contributed your shirt or your tea, you can
   look up where it grows and the climate it prefers. You
   may learn about time-honored woodworking methods,
   how garments traverse the globe in their journey to your
   closet, and the ancient intricacies of making tea. Creating these intentional narratives about our objects can
   help us think about the interconnectedness of the world,
   remind us how deeply embedded we are in nature, and
   encourage us to be more mindful about how we live and
   what we choose to surround ourselves with.

5

A HUMAN HISTORY OF HOUSEPLANTS

Shall I not have intelligence with the earth?
Am I not partly leaves and vegetable mould myself?

—Henry David Thoreau

. . . .

*"Plants are life. I love that I can take care and give
back to the earth. . . . Watching them grow, tending to
them, I've begun to connect with them; I could not
imagine my life without them."* —Cheyenne

I t's my hope that, by now, you're convinced that cultivating your own personal green space—wherever you live—will endow your life with benefits, from improved mental health to higher reserves of conscientiousness and compassion. But where to start?

As with anything new, it's ok to start small. Most people don't think this way, but the fact is, if you actively care for and learn from even just one plant, you're likely on the path to becoming a proficient gardener. In his book *Atomic Habits*, James Clear explains how your habits build your identity. We often become hyper-focused on outcomes, like the outcome of filling our home with plants. This is the wrong mind-set, though, he says. "Many people begin the process of changing their habits by focusing on *what* they want to achieve. This leads to outcome-based habits. The alternative is to build identity-based habits. With this approach, we start by focusing on *who* we want to become."

Similarly to Clear, I often share with people that as exciting as getting to the metaphorical summit of a mountain can be, what makes it so fulfilling is the journey. It's on that journey that you learn to overcome challenges and practice resilience. If you were just helicoptered onto the top of the mountain, you might enjoy the view, but you would have forgone all the experience you would have developed on the hike up. And by embarking on that journey, you develop skills that are transferrable to everyday life and that will in turn become part of a healthy routine. So the best way to build a routine—and therefore an identity as a gardener—is to look after, observe, and nurture just one plant, and grow from there. This means there's no need to focus on aesthetics—there's no rush to fill your house with plants, start an Instagram account, or lament over the fact that your house doesn't yet look like the leafiest of Pinterest boards. You're in this for the journey. The eventual outcomes will be like seeing the long-awaited bloom of a most challenging plant.

"One plant can make me a gardener?" you may exclaim. As it has been said, no leaf will ever replace the beauty of autumn; and a houseplant will never replace the beauty and grandeur of an intact ecosystem. And those reading this book who have sat with seedlings on their sills, built raised beds with bare hands, hoofed heaps of composted manure to vegetable beds, and wept over the loss of lettuce through endless skirmishes with slugs may roll their eyes at such a claim. The reality, however, is that the less time we spend in nature, the fewer interactions we have with her, so the best bet to begin having that conversation—or maintaining that connection with nature—may very well be through something as humble as a houseplant. Many in my community have found this to be true:

> "I grew up with a father who showed me the outdoors, and
> I found peace within nature. I find that being surrounded
> by plants within my own home brings me the same feeling

as standing barefoot in the woods and allows me to nurture what I otherwise cannot." —Aurelia L.

"Plants are something that I have been around my whole life, having both my parents as avid outdoor gardeners and growing up on a farm. When I moved to the city, however, I was a bit lost. I fell into five years of depression and anxiety; I felt I had no hobbies, no direction. It wasn't until last year that I discovered how satisfying nurturing a houseplant is. . . . I am studying to be a naturopath, and for me, connection to nature is so fundamental to mental and physical health. I realized, and am realizing more and more every day, that this is what I and most of us are missing in our lives!" —Sophie

"After my divorce, I ended up with burnout and four kids to care for. I took up barefoot running, as being in the woods and surrounded by nature made me feel revived. Sadly, during one of these sessions I suffered a spine injury and from that point was unable to stand up or walk for longer than a few minutes. Running, or going to the woods, [is] no longer in my power. Then I got into houseplants and decided that if I couldn't go to the jungle, I'd bring the jungle to me! Now I'm caring for about fifty plants. It makes me so happy. I feel alive again!" —Tamara

Messages like these from my community reveal the comforting truth that the relationship between a gardener and her plants is by no means one-sided. Yes, bringing plants into our homes requires from us consideration and care, but plants have a quiet, intuitive way of returning the love. Wrapped up in the identity of a gardener, then, is a touchpoint for inner peace.

Let me state the obvious: the "houseplant" is a human construct—something invented as we began to build four walls around us. Even though the idea of "domesticated" plants is fairly new, the idea of cultivating unusual or interesting plants is anything but new for us humans. This means that care for plants has largely been the same for millennia. By looking back through our history with plants, perhaps we can learn something from those who came before us.

Taking a piece of Eden with us

For the most part, the first gardeners were women. As early as 10,000 BC, it was females who foraged and tended to the forest, intuiting which plants were useful to their needs, including edible, ceremonial, and medicinal plants. Depending on where you look, men were not too far from the garden either—likely helping clear the land and, in some cases, tending to certain crops as well. In some traditional Amazonian cultures, for instance, men have long tended to the coca (*Erythroxylum* sp.), while women have long tended to the manioc (*Manihot esculenta*)—two of the most important "male" and "female" crops, respectively.

As nomadism in certain cultures ceased, gardening became even more popular. The first gardens were made out of necessity but often had deeply spiritual contexts as well; everything from the origin of seeds to the direction a garden was sown was rich in meaning and metaphor. The garden often mapped a culture's cosmology and origins, promoting strength of purpose, identity, and gratitude among a people. In the instance of coca and manioc mentioned prior, the pattern the crops are usually planted in signifies a bone-flesh relationship, with the coca resembling a skeletal human form and the manioc covering it to make a circular garden shape.

Some of the most exquisite gardens originated in Asia. Gardens in China were epic landscapes commissioned and used by royal families, and they have been documented going back about 3,600 years. Those gardens later inspired the art of Japanese gardening. Houseplant origins, however, can be traced to over 3,500 years ago, etched in stone by ancient Egyptians, Assyrians, and Sumerians. Though the existence of the Hanging Gardens of Babylon, an almost mythical tiered garden that is considered one of the Seven Wonders of the Ancient World, has been debated due to a lack of archaeological evidence, Oxford University Assyriologist Stephanie Dalley has presented some compelling archaeological and historical clues that the actual gardens did exist. Dalley posits that they were 340 miles (547 kilometers) north of Babylon in Nineveh and were constructed and executed by Sennacherib, an Assyrian king who reigned between 705 and 681 BC. Though much of the area, which is near the tumultuous city of Mosul, has been destroyed, the etchings that depict the garden, one of which is housed in the British Museum, would stir the imagination of any plant lover. The area would have featured vaulted, stadium-style architecture interspersed with pendulous plants, fruit-filled orchards, and magnificently large trees, creating an impressive indoor-outdoor architectural plantscape that we may now only see an approximation of in modern-day Singapore's recent plants-on-building designs and innovations. It is no exaggeration to say that the first houseplants were almost too beautiful to be true.

The Greek and Roman empires similarly adored plants, and they likely practiced gardening in pots and planters to worship their gods. It's also been documented that the first "greenhouse," known as a *specularium*, was developed during the reign of Roman emperor Tiberius (42 BC–37 AD). There was no such thing as sheet glass during this time, so instead, the greenhouse was fabricated with small translucent sheets of mica and kept warm with animal dung and fires burned along the sides. As such, Tiberius enjoyed year-round fruits, though it's been said that Seneca, a Roman philosopher, condemned such behavior, believing the forcing of plants to fruit and flower was against nature. After the fall of the Roman Empire, it was likely monks in cloister gardens who carried on the tradition of planting both indoors and out, particularly valuing medicinal varieties over anything else.

In the sixteenth and seventeenth centuries, serious plant hunters began to emerge from Europe, spawned by the desires of kings and queens to fill their gardens, much in the same way that Sennacherib desired 2,400 years earlier. The first wooden greenhouse was also built around this time, by Jacob Bobart the younger (1641–1719) at Oxford University Botanic Garden in 1670, and was heated by burning baskets of charcoal. Later greenhouses were heated by stoves, which earned the plants growing in these conditions the moniker "stove plants." Around this time, texts began to emerge on medicinal plants from the New World and about rich flora from "undiscovered" worlds, and extensive herbarium collections were being assembled to document the discovery of new plant species.

I wanted to see how our relationship with plants was being documented and discussed through time, so I took a bus upstate back to my alma mater, Cornell University. I never spent time at the Liberty Hyde Bailey Hortorium while I was going to school, but I would have if I'd known what a gem it was! While there, I met plant biologists Dr. William Crepet and Dr. Anna Stalter—the Hortorium's associate curator and extension botanist—and Peter Fraissinet, assistant curator and librarian.

The Bailey Hortorium, named after intrepid botanist, taxonomist, and horticulturalist Liberty Hyde Bailey, houses a collection of botanical books and journals, many of which were part of Bailey's own library while he was still alive. Since its founding, the collection has grown to approximately 30,000 volumes, 200 journal titles, and 900,000 botanical specimens housed in an herbarium.

In the herbarium, I dutifully followed Anna, whose salt-and-pepper hair matched the gray and white floral-print blouse she wore. We walked down tiled rows lined with gray steel–herbarium cabinets running the length of the room, her comfy sandals and my sneakers making a slight shuffling sound as we would stop and read the names on the cabinets.

Anna spun the large black handles of the cabinets and carefully pulled out page after page of botanical specimens. The mounted plants, which are often pressed to reveal the plant's main morphological characteristics, are labeled with scientific names, where the plant was collected, and who it was collected by. If the collector was thorough and unrushed, then he or she would include other detailed information—like how the plant was growing, where it was growing, and any other special characteristics of the plant and its surroundings. She showed me dainty ferns collected from upstate New

York; flattened cacti, spines and all, from Ecuador; pressed flowers from schoolkids—during a time when botany must have been deemed an important subject in schools; and even precious pressed plants from Captain Cook's voyages in the 1700s. Looking through all the specimens made me realize the joy of discovery many of these collectors must have experienced—not to mention the lengths that some would go to find, document, and understand the wondrous world of plants and share that with the rest of the world. (Admittedly, I know the feeling!)

Herbarium collections are filed by family name, so I asked Anna if she could show me *Araceae*, which include genera like *Philodendron* and *Monstera*—two popular kinds of houseplants. We wove our way through the monochromatic aisles, Anna scanning the names of the cabinets. "Here we are," she chirped. She pulled out a box of cream-colored archival pages bloated and bent from years of botanists unsuccessfully trying to press large fruits and inflorescences to a page. I could smell the naphthalene, which had been used in years past to preserve specimens from the errant insect. I asked to see a *Monstera punctulata*, a plant native to Mexico and Central America, denoted by impressively deep fenestrations, or "windows," on its leaves. The specimen, which had been collected on a tree growing by a roadside, according to the collector's notes, barely fit on a page, folded over itself—as crisp as an overly starched, tattered suit. It was collected by "G. S. Bunting" on September 21, 1961. I later found out the collector was George Sydney Bunting, a botanist who had passed in just 2015 and was well-known for his extensive work on cultivated aroids, which is a family of plants that includes *Philodendron*, *Monstera*, and other common household varieties like *Aglaonema* and *Spathiphyllum*. I could imagine the botanist's excitement when spotting the plant. "Stop the car!" I could hear him say, before pulling over to the side of the highway to climb the slope to collect it. It is no doubt the same kind of excitement that I—and others—get when seeing and discovering a new plant for the first time.

Anna and I continued on with our perusal of the herbarium. She, of course, was familiar with each plant, but just by observing her facial expressions, you could tell that she didn't tire of showing them. I'd imagine her enthusiasm was a reflection of the unbridled excitement and appreciation of the person whom she was showing around. She stopped at an herbarium cabinet with shelves and pulled out not a pressed page, but a box, which was big enough to fit a basketball player's shoes. In some cases, seeds and other items were so uncooperative in being pressed between their two-dimensional pages that they instead required a larger home. Here, she said, was the seed from the *Lodoicea* tree, which is endemic to the Seychelles. The seed, which looks like a tight, polished brown buttocks (if I can be so brash) is the largest seed in the world. The plant that produces this seed was called *coco de mer*, or coconut of the sea, because explorers saw its seeds floating in the ocean miles from land and figured they were born of trees in a layer of earth deep beneath the ocean's depths. I marveled over the seed's sheer size and structure.

Though these collections can seem outmoded and out of step with modern times, they prove to be quite useful across a range of disciplines. They not only preserve a piece of our botanical history but also help today's botanists and scientists analyze previous geographic ranges of certain plant species—to understand how much habitat has been gained or, in most cases, lost over time. Furthermore, scientists can use the specimens to identify plants, or resolve taxonomic disputes, which invariably happen. Additionally, herbarium specimens act as a source of DNA that scientists can extract for their studies. And lastly, specimens can also serve as a useful reference for botanic gardens, growers, and houseplant owners to consult when trying to figure out a plant's optimum growing conditions. If you ever have a chance to step into an herbarium, I would encourage it, as it's like seeing a rich museum of plants—giving you an opportunity to transport back into the shoes of the botanist or explorer who collected, documented, and pressed the plant.

Of course, not all plants wind up pressed between pages; some have different destinies—winding up in botanic gardens' and collectors' glasshouses, gardens, and private collections—and in some cases are direct-line predecessors of the plants we grow today.

"I have that *Rhaphidophora cryptantha*," I once said to Chad Husby, botanical horticulturist at the Fairchild Tropical Botanic Garden in Florida, pointing to a shingling plant splayed out on the well-shaded wall. "It could be that yours is a descendent, because this one came to Fairchild in the 1970s from a botanic garden in New Guinea," he replied. "It turned out it was an undescribed species at that time." Though still uncommon because of how slowly it grows, the *Rhaphidophora* has made it into the houseplant market. Two of them now reside in my home.

While Anna and I were busying ourselves in herbarium specimens, Peter emerged from the basement with a series of old botanical tomes. If I thought Anna was delicate with the herbarium specimens, Peter was more so with the books, some of which were nearly 400 years old. He laid books out like a mosaic of leather-bound tiles across the table. I, too scared to approach the books for their apparent frailty, was encouraged by a nod from Peter. I gingerly thumbed through each historic book, each meticulously researched and written by its author. Some books were well preserved—thick, yellowed-edged pages bound by worn calfskin covers that carried the scent of times past. Others had pages as delicate as moth wings, so thin and so frail that certain pages and their tattooed inscriptions had worn threadbare. Almost all were illustrated with the finest engravings, showing charmingly detailed elements of plants and their anatomy.

While at Cornell, I came across books written by plantspeople of the past, one of whom is especially relevant to modern-day plant lovers. In the summer of 1829, a medical doctor, Nathaniel Bagshaw Ward, had happened upon a discovery that led to higher plant survival both on ships and in homes.

His story of discovery starts with a grand gardening failure, which should make all of us who have lost plants feel a little more at ease. Much in the way that I sought to build an indoor vertical garden for my home after reading the work of French botanist Patrick Blanc, Ward had attempted to build his own wall of moss and ferns, interspersing the creation with primroses, wood sorrel, and other plants he found in the surrounding area. In short, his plants soon perished, which he claimed was a consequence of the smoke from nearby manufacturing—a logical assumption, particularly since photosynthesis (and therefore growth) halts with enough particulate matter in the air.

Whatever the reason for failure, Ward resorted to other pursuits, one of which was burying a chrysalis of a sphinx moth in some moist soil contained in a wide-mouthed glass bottle, covered with a lid. During this period, he saw how the moisture condensed on the surface of glass, returning to the soil, so a degree of moisture and humidity remained in the jar. It was then that he made his grand observation, written of here:

> About a week prior to the final change of the insect, a seedling fern and a grass made their appearance on the surface of the mould [soil].
>
> I could not but be struck with the circumstance of one of that very tribe of plants which I had for years fruitlessly attempted to cultivate, coming up *sponte suâ* in such a situation, and asked myself seriously what were the conditions necessary for its well-being? To this the reply was—*a moist atmosphere free from soot or other extraneous particles; light; heat; moisture; periods of rest;* and *change of air.* All these my plant had; *the circulation of air* being obtained by the diffusion law already described.
>
> Thus, then, *all the conditions* requisite for the growth of my fern were apparently fulfilled, and it remained only to test the fact by experiment. I placed the bottle outside the window of my study, a room with a northern aspect, and to my great delight the plants continued to thrive. They turned out to be *L. Filix mas* and the *Poa annua.* They required no attention of any kind, and there they remained for nearly four years, the grass once flowering, and the fern producing three or four fronds annually. At the end of this time they accidentally perished, during my absence from home, in consequence of the rusting of the lid, and the consequent too free admission of rain water.

Given that Ward spent time to observe the needs of the plants, he (perhaps) unknowingly landed on what would be a novel idea of the time, which was to enclose plants in glass, and would in turn ultimately lead to an influx of foreign plants into Europe and eventually the United States. His idea was later called the Wardian case (our modern-day terrarium), which he codified in his book, *On the Growth of Plants in Closely Glazed Cases*, written first in 1842 and then later published in a second volume in 1852. He admits that already by the time he wrote his book "the conveyance of plants on shipboard . . . is now universally adopted, and it is believed that there is not a civilized spot upon the earth's surface which has not, more or less, benefited by their [the Wardian cases'] introduction." The purpose of writing his book, however, was not to toot his own horn, but to guide people on how to care for plants within closed cases, as he clearly recognized that plant care was still so poorly understood. He realized that you couldn't just put a plant in some soil in a glass case and neglect any or all the other elements that a plant needs, like light, water, humidity, airflow, and more. The same goes for plants in the home, which of course we'll touch upon.

Though Ward was already well-known by the time his book was published, he still was unlikely to reach all plant-interested people with his message. Nonetheless, his creation unequivocally stimulated the public interest and fervor for living with plants, particularly in city areas that were increasingly being described as fuliginous due to heavy pollution. More books on house, parlor, greenhouse, and "stove" plants (the latter named because they literally required potbellied stoves in greenhouses to be kept alive) began to proliferate in the mid-1800s, with titles such as *Flowers for the*

Parlor and Garden, *House Plants and How to Grow Them*, *House Plants and How to Succeed with Them*, *The Window Flower Garden*, *Window Gardening*, and a host of other deliberately descriptive names. Though some of the texts are over 150 years old now, they are definitively modern—with many elements of plant care, design, and even enthusiasm still relevant today.

As the Victorian era ended and we moved into the 1900s, tropical nurseries and greenhouses in the Northeast, California, and Florida began to emerge to satisfy a plant lover's itch; their catalogs began to cater not just to people's interests in outdoor varieties, like flowers, trees, and shrubs, but also to the growing desire to have foliage plants in homes and in private conservatories.

These plants included common varieties that we know today, like *Aglaonema*, *Dracaena*, and *Howea*, for example, but also a wealth of lesser-known species, many of which I would certainly get excited about if they showed up at my local plant shop. One such greenhouse, Roehrs, founded by a young man named Julius Roehrs, was established back in 1869 in East Rutherford, New Jersey, and is still in operation today. At the start of the greenhouse, Roehrs grew flowering plants for private customers and florist shops, the latter of which were starting to pop up in Manhattan. He sourced from all over—Burma, India, North Africa, South and Central America—and it was reputed that entire boatloads of plants from Europe would be consigned directly to "Julius Roehrs Co." At the height of Roehrs's operation—at least according to old catalogs at Cornell's hortorium—a wealthy greenhouse owner could have had his choice of several thousand different tropical varieties, largely collected by the German American botanist Alfred

Byrd Graf, who became associated with the Julius Roehrs Company in 1931.

The quest for more indoor plants picked up throughout the 1930s and again in the 1950s and has continued to steadily rise through the decades. The big plant boom happened in the mid-1970s and has been compared to the fervor indoor plants hold today. Nearly a third of houseplant sales are driven by Millennials, according to a 2018 article in *The New York Times*.

Since the 1970s, people throughout the world have begun moving to the cities at historic rates. This phenomenon, coupled with the excitement about plants recently fueled by social media, has amounted to a quiet yet competitive indoor-botanical culture. "Keeping up with the Joneses" used to just be about the neighbors who abutted our properties. But now inspiration—and aspiration— exists everywhere, in any place, just a social feed or hashtag away, connecting plant lovers and plant groups across the world. Of course, social media can be used (and is being used) to connect people with mutual interest in plants—and connect them to the (sometimes too picture-perfect) world of caring for plants. However, a curated view of our chlorophyllous companions shouldn't prevent us from adopting the same mind-set that gardeners before us had, asking ourselves, "What do plants need from me?"

In fact, as I write this book, I realize that I am catering to the contemporary plant lover or future plant lover, just as the authors of the books and the greenhouse owners who put out the catalogs I mentioned above did for the people of their time; and surely future authors will continue forward far beyond my time here on Earth.

Three-quarters of all American families use living plants as part of their home decor or cultural expression. This shows that house-plants have indeed become mainstream and that there is some level of knowledge around keeping plants. That being said, there's always more to learn, and part of making a plant love you is about understanding the considerations for growing plants indoors, which is what we'll explore more fully in the next chapters. We'll do this, however, by continually reframing the way we think about plants and by extending our imaginations to cast off our corporeal forms—at least temporarily—and fully delight in the immersive idea of what it must be like to be a plant.

GET-GROWING EXERCISE: DISCOVERY

1. **Discover a plant oasis.** Visit your local botanic garden or garden center, or choose a plant from your collection or one that interests you online. The easiest way to start building your mental map of plants is by learning about them one at a time.

2. **Uncover the history of how a plant came into cultivation.** Once a new plant species has captured your imagination, home in on its history. This may be a little challenging, so see if you can do a search for when it made it into botanical records, checking out online herbarium databases and science journals. If your plant is a hybrid or cultivar, see if you can discover when it was hybridized or cultivated and how long it's been in circulation.

3. See where it lives now. If you are able, see what plant sellers are currently keeping it in circulation. This exercise will help you get more familiar with the history of the plant in question—and its journey to become popular in the market—as well as help you decide whether you can make a happy home for it.

6

GETTING TO KNOW YOUR PLANTS

**Sometimes I wish I could photosynthesize so that just
by being, just by shimmering at the meadow's edge or
floating lazily on a pond, I could be doing the work
of the world while standing silent in the sun.**

—*Robin Wall Kimmerer,* Braiding Sweetgrass: Indigenous
Wisdom, Scientific Knowledge, and the Teachings of Plants

. . . .

*"The science of plants deeply fascinates me.
Plants have helped me find a deeper purpose." —Sarah A.*

Do you want a life or a lifestyle?

As we increasingly move to cities, our individual and collective experience and encounters with plants, particularly in their native habitats, diminish and dwindle. Instead of climbing trees, we may be putting a small bonsai in our grocery cart. Instead of learning to build soil from our food scraps, we may be purchasing potting medium in packages. Nature becomes sanitized, potted, packaged, and primped. Therefore, the more that we can get to know our plant, the more we can understand and appreciate its backstory and how it got to us in the first place.

In the previous chapter, we learned about humanity's fascination with and need to be around plants, how to begin identifying as a gardener by ingesting a bit of history, and reinforcing that identity by building habits. As we habituate ourselves to care properly for our plants, we ultimately deepen our relationship with the Earth. However, if we pay attention to only how our plants look in our home, the right habits may never form, and our relationship to the Earth will be only surface level. Developing a mind-set that encourages us to care for the needs of our plants will allow us to experience "plant love" instead of "plant lust," and a "life" instead of just a "lifestyle."

In order to build good caregiving habits, we need to first adopt a caregiving mind-set: this means being inquisitive, like noticing how a plant grows and the characteristics of its leaves, stems, and roots; learning where our plants come from; and figuring out what environments and conditions they thrive in—all before bringing them home. At first pass, learning about plants may not seem easy—and beginners will often be overwhelmed at the many varieties of plants and each of their needs. In this chapter, however, I'll begin to demystify plant care so that you're equipped to make the best decisions for you and your plant.

Meeting a plant for the first time is not so different from meeting a person for the first time. If we're good listeners and good conversationalists, then there's a better likelihood that we will get to know the person we're speaking with. The same principles go for our plants—except, as you have figured out, we need to hone different skills, since plants tell their stories and respond in very different ways. This often requires us to become more adept at doing some preliminary research, taking time to observe our plants, and even doing a little self-inquiry and reflection.

Ask where your plant is from

Especially if you live in a city, you may never think about what life was like for the plants you see on display, wrapped up in plastic or arranged into a bouquet, before they were curated on a shelf in your local market. Where were they grown? How long did it take to get them to a state where they could be sold? I began unearthing many of these questions while filming for my YouTube series, *Plant One On Me*, where I often interview hobby growers and private collectors, and visit large greenhouses and botanic gardens.

Cultivators of plants can spend up to a decade "perfecting" a plant before it even gets to market. By "perfecting," I mean selecting not only the fanciest foliage or blooms to entice us to buy them but also the plants that can withstand the rigors of shipping, shop neglect, and plant-owner folly. "You want a plant that will at least last three months in a plant owner's care," I've heard many growers say. In fact, I've heard that line so many times, I've questioned whether growers were reciting lines from the same manual. This just shows how little faith some growers have when it comes to the everyday consumer's ability to care for a plant!

Even if a houseplant was born, cultivated, or propagated in a nursery or greenhouse setting, it is still a species that once lived trailing, winding, or vining across a woodland clearing, clinging to rock outcrops or desert landscapes, or maybe even soaring high on branches in the rain forest canopy. Knowing more of the natural history of a plant is important, as it can help you understand what conditions it prefers and even why it grows the way it grows.

Plants' natural ecosystems may seem impossible to re-create in our home environments, but many of the 500 or so popular cultivated indoor-foliage varieties that we often see at greenhouses, nurseries, and plant shops are actually better adapted for home or office environments. To borrow an example from the animal kingdom, rock doves, also known as common pigeons, easily adapt to cityscapes and skyscrapers, seeing that they originally lived on

cliffs and rock ledges in the wild. Most houseplants that we see today are tropical and subtropical plants that originate in areas within
1,600 miles (2,575 kilometers) north—and within 1,600 miles south—
of the equator. Some are found in deserts, some are found clinging
to bare earth on mountainsides, and still others are commonly found
in dappled or low-light conditions in the understories of forests and
jungles throughout the world. Many of these plants have adapted to
conditions not too dissimilar from our home environments—at
least when it comes to the temperature we like to keep our homes at,
which is to say 65 to 70°F or 18 to 21°C. And still others, like certain
cacti and succulents, are used to neglect, so someone who is forgetful at watering or who travels a lot but has a sunny windowsill may
actually find a friend in a cactus or succulent.

Not so long ago, I was hiking through Tapantí National Park in
Costa Rica, about 30 miles (48.3 kilometers) southeast of San José,
and was ecstatic to see the fuzzy petioles, russet-stained undersides,
and velvety leaves of a *Philodendron verrucosum*; the fenestrated
leaves and creamsicle-cloaked inflorescence of a *Monstera* sp.; and
branches heavily laden with epiphytic *Tillandsia* sp. and bromeliads—
all specimens that are cornerstones in plant shops worldwide. It's
amazing how foreign places such as this can start feeling so familiar
when you simply notice their plants. And as you begin to surround
yourself with nature in your own home, you'll be surprised at how
inviting—and how strangely familiar—it will begin to feel.

This is not all to say that you need to turn your living room into
a jungle if your plants originated in one. However, knowing a little
more about your plants' natural history, like where they grow and
how they grow in their native environments, as well as how they
work, can surely help you help your plants grow and thrive.

Find out how plants work

Plants may seem physiologically simple compared to mammals, but they're actually comparably sophisticated. Over millions of years, plants have evolved to live in just about every situation, not only with their own kind, but with all kinds. They thrive, despite the elements, in snow-packed alpine ranges, desert landscapes, and rocky outcrops blistering in the sun. They have been and continue to be plagued and preyed upon by insects, fungi, bacteria, viruses, birds, animals, humans, and even other plants. They, as a whole, have learned to withstand forces of Biblical proportions, like heavy winds, floods, and fires; some plants, particularly those in seed stage, have even used these climatic disasters to their advantage—spreading their progeny far and wide in the aftermath of the tumult. Now that's far more than I can say for the human species!

Like a monk in meditation, plants are rooted to their place, but are anything but restful in their surroundings. What may be registered as "unmoving" to us is often a series of imperceptible (yet sometimes perceptible) movements and growth—aboveground, belowground, and even on a cellular level within leaves, stems, roots, and seeds. A plant's aboveground structures, though obvious, are still subtle in their ways. Plants responsive to us, say a *Mimosa pudica*, or sensitive plant, whose compound leaves fold inward as we stroke them; or a *Dionaea muscipula*, or Venus flytrap, which triggers a trap after two strokes of its bristles within twenty seconds of one another, are strange delights for young and old alike.

A plant's belowground structures, that is to say her roots, are even more mysterious. A dark cloak of soil or substrate surrounds the roots, propping a plant up and giving her the best supply of water, keeping her roots from becoming waterlogged. Roots and root hairs stretch and probe beneath the soil, like water witches, stealthily searching for moisture gradients. Plants are so attuned to their dark underground environment that it has even been shown that they may use acoustical vibrations—like the sound of running water—to dowse for water sources at a distance. Once they've detected moisture in the soil, they siphon both water and dissolved nutrients, via osmosis, from root hairs through stems and up to the crown in a process known as "ascent of sap." It's the dissolved nutrients—or *cations*—like magnesium, phosphorus, and nitrogen that become part of the plant tissue and aid the plant in important life functions like enzyme production and metabolism. These nutritious benefits are then bestowed onto those who eat plants, including humans. And yet, many humans have never noticed these life-giving benefits, but perhaps we'll feel more grateful for them the next time we eat our vegetables.

Plants are the connective tissue between earth and sky. As water makes its way up through the plant, it exits the leaves, and in some cases the stems, through small lips-shaped pores called *stomata*; this process is called transpiration. This gaseous exhalation from the leaves creates humidity in the surrounding atmosphere—both indoors and out—and fuels the water cycle, which indigenous peoples of the Amazon describe as "rivers in the sky." This moisture eventually gathers in clouds and falls to earth again, ensuring that plants of all kinds have a reliable source of water.

The stomata also create a pathway for both carbon dioxide and oxygen to pass freely into and out of the plant. As CO_2 comes in, the carbon is cleaved by light energy and combines with water to yield carbohydrates, oxygen, and residual water. The light energy that fuels this whole process is captured by the green part of the plant—the chlorophyll—which is found in the leaves and stems. A plant's leaves are intricately and efficiently designed to consume light, acting like giant solar panels that can track the sun's movements throughout the day and over time, giving the plant a reliable energy source to fuel itself—and to fuel the world. In the winter months or dry seasons, when many plants go dormant, they shuttle the carbohydrates down through the stem to be stored in their roots and modified root systems like tubers, corms, bulbs, and rhizomes. When springtime or the rainy season comes, the plants can pull the carbohydrate stores up again, which is why we can tap maples for syrup in spring and sweet potatoes can generate such prolific green growth from their tubers on our kitchen counters.

As you begin to appreciate the subtleties of plants, not only will you learn about how to care for them but you'll also begin to consider the pace of their lives. Plants are slow, quiet, and, most of all, complex creatures. As you bring them into your life, I encourage you to match their disposition when you can. By developing this sensitivity toward plants, you may find that the more you give to plants, the more you gain. With practice, it'll start to come naturally:

> "Because of my chronic pain, I often can't take part in life as much as I'd like. It's also one of the reasons why I don't have animals at the moment, but plants bring an aliveness in my life that's very compatible with my limitations. I identify with them so much, and this definitely has to do with overcoming adversity." —Tove T.

"I've been gardening for five years now. . . . When I'm struggling mentally, I neglect my plant babies without even realizing it, which makes me realize the state I'm in, and I immediately go to care for my plants while they care for me. It's been a lovely process." —Anna Morgan R.

"I am a freelance creative, so I find that I have a lot of ups and downs. What has really helped with this roller coaster are my plants. Every day I tend to them, which gives me a regular ritual of care. I've found that through this, it has not only calmed my nerves and anxiety, but has also allowed me to better understand them, too." —Todd

Sunday is my plant sabbath. I'll tell you more about it later, but it's my day to slow down and care for each of my plants. This ritual not only keeps them healthy—it keeps *me* healthy. These stories from my community are proof that slowing down could help you to heal, whether from physical sickness, the inevitable daily stressors of modern life, or a broken heart.

Ask what plant wants to live with you

"That's a beautiful *Maranta*," I said to the young man walking out of the plant shop near my house.

He paused. "What did you call it?"

"A *Maranta*," I repeated. "It's commonly known as a prayer plant."

"Oh, cool," he said. "I had no idea what it was. I bought it 'cause I liked the look of it."

He didn't turn to leave right away, so I quickly gave him a Cliffs Notes version of prayer plant care tips, trying to choose words that he could potentially understand and remember. "It likes some bright light, but no direct sun, and prefers a humid environment. You'll see its leaves fold up during the evening hours, as if in prayer, which is how it got its name."

By the time I finished my sentence, his shoulders were already halfway turned in the other direction. He exchanged a cursory "thank you" and was on his way with his *Maranta leuconeura* var. *erythroneura*. (Try to say that ten times fast!)

I've lived next to a plant shop for long enough (more than twelve years), spent enough time giving workshops, and traveled in and out of enough garden centers and plant stores to engage in and eavesdrop on plenty of conversations. Most times, I find people wander into plant shops, knowing very little about plants, and come out buying something they think will look good "right there" (meaning, in a specific space in their house), without any knowledge of whether it's the appropriate kind of plant for the space or even for the person. Additionally, having lived in the city now for fourteen years, I've found that apartment living is often compromised: short on space, on light, on humidity—and on airflow. As such, one of the more common inquiries from aspirant urban plant owners is, "What plant is hard to kill?"

I want to get there by positing a different question—one that will shift the way you approach buying plants altogether. Next time you go to a plant shop, or purchase a plant online, don't just ask what plant you'd like to live with, but ask what plant would like to live with you. We often buy a plant based on aesthetics and say things like, "Don't you think that will be perfect for the corner of the bedroom?" but fail to ask whether a plant will thrive in that corner of the bedroom—let alone survive. Additionally, we may yearn for the most high-maintenance species in the plant shop but may find ourselves to be relatively "hands-off" when it comes to plant care. These two characteristics don't work together, likely only resulting in an unhappy plant and therefore an unhappy plant owner. So, in summary, ask first what a plant wants from you, and then see if that matches up with not only what you want but also what you can provide the plant to ensure it remains happy under your care.

It's natural for us to want to surround ourselves with nature, but it's often exhausting to learn how nature works and incorporate that knowledge into our lives. When we create such a distinct and radical separation between "outside" and "in," it almost feels necessary to bring the beauty of nature into our homes and onto our balconies. Building indoor waterfalls and bringing bird nests into one's home, as I did as a child, is one thing; but when you begin to adorn your home with plants, that's another: there's a bit of a learning curve, but one that's easily overcome as we familiarize ourselves with our individual plant's needs.

Plants have the miraculous ability to "perk up" a place effortlessly. They literally and figuratively bring life to a space because they *are* life. This may seem to be the most obvious statement in the book, but it warrants repeating: Plants. Are. Life. They exude life because they are growing, moving, breathing, and metabolizing—and we have to do our part to ensure they stay that way. Though these processes may differ substantially from the ways a human grows, moves, breathes, and metabolizes, they are inarguably connected enough for us to understand them. Fill an empty space with a hundred partygoers and the atmosphere is brought to life. Fill that same empty space with a hundred meditators and that space is again brought to life, albeit in a different way. Fill that same empty space with a hundred rooted plants, and no one will argue: that space is indeed alive! But don't just take it from me:

"I'm from a small town and grew up with plenty of nature around me. After college, however, I moved to the city and now live in a tiny shoebox apartment with literally no outdoor space. Luckily, my bedroom has a big picture window, so I put some plants in there. As soon as I brought them indoors, I felt better and the room felt so alive. My roommate enjoyed the way they looked too, so I have her hooked and now she's growing plants in her bedroom!"
—Zuzanna S.

"My mom passed away a week before I started college. I felt very lost and alone until I discovered horticulture. Not only is placing my hands in the dirt unbelievably therapeutic, incorporating plants into my home made it feel much less lonely. They're so calming to me, both because they make the space [look] nicer and because it makes me feel good to watch a living thing I care for flourish!" —Meag Sargent

"I used to buy plants because I liked how they looked. When they died (and they *all* died), I'd just throw them away. This may sound odd, but I never thought about caring for them throughout their life. I guess I just looked at them as a disposable décor item. But as I started to see others on social media having a good time caring for their plants, it occurred to me that I was really missing the point. Now that I have a new perspective, caring for plants has become my favorite hobby." —Josef

Plants are life. This means that, if we listen to their needs closely enough, we can make space for them to fill the voids inside our souls. This may sound strange or even cheesy, but I believe that one of the most natural functions of both plants and humans is to care for and comfort—to bring life to—one another. There was a time when this relationship was more apparent, but since society has re-organized itself around industry, we look to products and packaging to fill our voids. This book, in part, is a call to join me and my community to turn back the clocks and return to a slower time, even if just for a few hours every Sunday.

GET-GROWING EXERCISE: GO ON A PLANT DATE

Now that you've gotten a solid frame of mind to approach plant care, it's time to get to know your plant better. Just like when you go on a date, the plant sitting across from you at the garden shop may not be the right one for you (e.g., it's nice to look at, but very high maintenance), so you just have to find that out by asking the right questions! Take one plant that you have been eyeing and before you buy it, go through the following queries:

1. **Ask where your plant is from:** Once you've learned the plant's name, do a little more research on it and see where it originates and in what kind of ecosystem it lives. What can you deduce from that? (E.g., a plant that grows in the understories of the tropical forests of Ecuador may be tolerant of lower light conditions.)

2. **Find out how the plant works:** What does the plant look like? Examine it thoroughly. For instance, is it rootless or does it have fine roots, fleshy roots, or perhaps a tuber or a bulb? A plant with no roots, like many *Tillandsia*, may require foliar misting or soaking, whereas a plant with a tuber or bulb may go dormant during part of the year and require no water whatsoever in its dormancy. Finding out how your particular plant works will help you see if you can better care for it.

3. **Ask whether the plant would like to live with you:** Once you have a keen sense of where the plant is from and how it works, ask whether the plant would thrive in your home and under your care. That will help give you an indication as to whether you should consider a next "date" with your plant.

7

HOW TO MAKE A PLANT LOVE YOU

The garden is where you take the time in your life to tune in and
listen. It just takes being still long enough, opening your heart,
opening your spirit up to what the plants have to tell you.

—Gabriel Howearth, permaculturalist and botanist

. . . .

*"When I began looking at plants as living beings—
giving them love and respect—that's when I realized how
nourishing to the soul they can be." —Monica K.*

y friend Tama Matsuoka Wong is a pro forager who harvests wild greens, herbs, spices, and vegetables for high-end restaurants. I was surprised when she confessed she was a terrible gardener. Well, I was surprised she was so hard on herself. As a forager, she doesn't have to have a green thumb—just a good eye. Nature does the growing for her!

Tama is certainly an expert in one thing: knowing why plants grow well in certain locations. She appreciates the fact that plants often grow best where you find them—and sometimes where you don't want them (e.g., weeds). Noticing this is part of getting to know and understanding plants. If we take the next step to garden with them—whether indoors or out—we may need to ask things like, "What environment can I create for them so they can truly thrive?"

Tama points out that some botanists have a word for plants whose new parents have taken them home without considering what they need to thrive: *prisoners of war*. Prisoner-of-war plants are confined in planters or cages, and fertilized and watered in order to be kept alive. "If you really want to say that the plant is doing well and thriving, then is it regenerating?" Tama asked. "If not, then it's probably a prisoner-of-war plant."

If one of a plant's imperatives is to regenerate, producing off-shoots or pollinating to produce new seeds, for example, then we must ask ourselves what a plant requires to best thrive in the environment we have. But it's about more than just water and light (though getting those right is huge!); in order for a plant to love you, you may need to fill in for Mother Nature. And since most of our plants are in planters, they do not have the benefit of falling leaves from the forest canopy, fungal symbioses, or a soupy mix of microbes and other beneficial soil organisms like earthworms. This means that a plant owner will often find herself tending to her plant's every need—from finding the best light for her plant to aerating the soil with some chopsticks.

Author Stephen Harrod Buhner has written, "[Plants] are a life-form rooted in and identified by their community, by their relationships to and interactions with all other life on Earth." Plants, he argues, are "nothing in isolation." Though I empathize with Buhner's statements, I know we may never be able to fully re-create the intricacies and complexities of nature's ecosystems inside our homes, but I do believe the very act of growing can help connect us to something much larger.

As I've shown, even a plant in isolation can be a portal into something much greater, acting as a delegate or symbol of where it had originally come from. How they look, the way they grow, and their very physiology can give us insights into the environment from whence they came. If we are patient and fortunate enough to develop a sensitivity toward plants, then we can not only care for them with greater acuity but also reconnect to our origins, develop a deeper respect for nature, and ultimately reaffirm our role as stewards of our environment—so that our environment can take care of us. By helping plants reach their fullest potential, we can perhaps reach ours! Yes, indoors will never be a substitute for nature, but there are certainly steps you can take to re-create a plant's natural home, and help it to not only survive—but thrive. In this penultimate chapter, we'll explore some of the major elements of what a plant needs so we can better prepare for bringing them into our lives and homes.

Plants and light

"Why are plants green?"

When my friend's three-year-old son asked me this, my friend's lips flattened into a shallow frown as if to ask, "You got this?"

"Why don't you ask the plant?" I responded.

"Plants don't talk!" he squealed, laughing and throwing his chubby hands in the air.

"That's what you think!" I countered. "My plants talk to me, but they do so in their own quiet way, so instead of asking a question out loud, you have to instead sit and observe."

This little boy's question reminded me that something so ubiquitous—that is to say, the "greenness" of a plant—is not only surprisingly complex but crucial to its survival. The simplest answer to his question is that they produce a pigment called *chlorophyll*. And chlorophyll is green because of the central ion of magnesium, which makes the chlorophyll molecule functional. If you've ever seen a meteor fall to earth that appears a green or teal color, it's because it is made mostly of magnesium. (This also explains why leaves turn yellow when they have a magnesium deficiency. No magnesium, no green—a subject more for my Houseplant Masterclass than for this book.) The chlorophyll in a plant is designed to absorb all visible light wavelengths—particularly in the red and blue ends of the spectrum. Since the green wavelength isn't utilized as much, it's that wavelength that is reflected back into our eye. Hence why plants are green.

A plant's greenness is therefore often a sign that it is healthy and thriving. There may be only a few tiny corners, if any, in your home through which sunlight enters, and that will help dictate where you may need to place your plant, as it needs to eat the light to grow, produce, and regenerate. South-facing windows in the Northern Hemisphere, if unobstructed, provide high-light areas, perfectly suitable for cacti, most succulents, and even herbs. Plants less tolerant to such a barrage of sun—often those with thin, delicate leaves—will often experience leaf damage, as they don't have protection against the harsh rays. Western and eastern exposures in the Northern Hemisphere provide great light for most plants, though true western windows can provide too-hot sun in the afternoon, which can scorch some plants. A northern aspect often gives just gentle, indirect light, ideal for low-light-tolerant varieties. If you understand the type of light your home provides and a plant's light needs, you can surely find one for which you can make a happy home.

When you cut off light to a plant, however, you cut off its very food source. Even *achlorophyllous* plants (plants that contain no chlorophyll), which often grow in the darkest depths of a forest, *need* to get their sustenance—indirectly—from light. The parasitic Indian pipe (*Monotropa uniflora*), a waxy, ethereal plant that looks as if it was dreamed up for one of Tim Burton's macabre films, is such an organism. I recall the first time I saw Indian pipe. I had been playing in a woodland adjacent to my home in Pennsylvania, as I had often done every weekend, and was riveted with my own discovery of such an unusual plant. I knew exactly what it was—largely owing to my visual memorization of every field guide I owned. That being said, I didn't know *why* it was.

Plants get crafty about their sun needs

Monotropa uniflora is one of 3,000 species of nonphotosynthetic flowering plants that can survive without any light. It lives in the darkness of the forest floor, and is pretty much impossible to grow inside your home (as a kid, I tried and failed!); it ultimately "saps" energy from chlorophyll-producing plants via underground mycorrhizal networks of fungi, earning it the name "mycoheterotroph." The ghostly Indian pipe, whose waxy white flower head hangs down, slumped on its equally white stem, as if it were noosed, taps its roots into the webby, white filaments festooned between trees and fungi, such as those in the genera *Russula* and *Lactarius*. Without the beech (*Fagus* sp.) and hemlock (*Tsuga* sp.) trees, with their ability to photosynthesize, and fungus, with its ability to siphon and shuttle nutrients—and arguably without the rest of the forest ecosystem—you can't grow Indian pipe.

But not unlike Indian pipe's clever ways to extract what it needs, photosynthetic plants have all sorts of tricks "up their leaves" in order to sop up energy from the sun's rays. They can position their leaves toward the sun, like movable solar panels; they can increase growth of their stems so they can reach a faraway light source (hence why some plants get "leggy"—a term that describes elongated stems as the plant's terminal leaves search for a suitable source of light); and they can even shift around the sun-eating organelles inside their leaves to maximize light intake. Light is so vital to helping a plant thrive that its rate of growth is proportional to the intensity, quality, quantity, and even timing of the light that it receives. So considering light is an important first order of business for growing a plant indoors.

TOO MUCH OF A GOOD THING

Some people may think that giving plants more light is beneficial, reasoning that more light equals more food for the plants, but that's not always the case. It is certainly possible for plants to get too much sun. Just like people, plants can burn in the UV rays, some more easily than others. Plants that live in hot, harsh terrains have adapted to minimize their light intake or protect their cells from the intense rays of the sun. Adaptations include reflective, thick cuticular leaves; white, woolly hairs; the production of natural sunscreen made of anthocyanins, which is akin to our melanin; and a host of other protections. Some plants that can withstand such sun intensity include *Mammillaria*, *Echeveria*, *Crassula*, *Opuntia*, and *Tephrocactus*.

Next time you buy a plant, take a good look at its leaves, stems, and even its form; imagine for a few moments what type of environment it came from. And before choosing a plant that you really want, consider the light conditions of your apartment, house, or room first. Then narrow down your choices from there. If the lighting requirements are not listed on a plant, you can always ask a nursery or plant store representative for advice.

Plants and water

You already know that plants are dependent on water. And how often you water a plant in the home will primarily depend on the quality and quantity of light that you give it, though there are other factors that come into account, like the type of plant, the moisture in the air (i.e., humidity), and how well-draining the substrate is, for example.

Some plants, like ferns, need more water than others. If you get a low-maintenance cactus because you're forgetful at watering, keep in mind that even desert-living plants, like most cacti and succulents, eventually need to be watered. When my friend and colleague Allan Schwarz—the architect and forest conservationist in Mozambique whom I mentioned earlier—visited me, he was bemused by my *Lithops*. These pebble-like succulents sat in khaki-colored coffee mugs on my windowsill. He had never seen a domesticated *kaitjie-kloukie*, as he called them. (The name, which in the local South African dialect Afrikaans means "kitten's paw," is derived from their resemblance to the soft pads of a kitten's feet.) He told me about the first time he had met these strange plants, while serving in the South African army.

In the eighties, he was stationed in Namaqualand, an inhospitably arid region of Namibia and South Africa. Rainfall in the area is parsimonious, but during his time there, a rare but welcoming rain had passed through; the next morning in between trainings, he happened upon what looked like a smooth, colorful pebble. He went to pick it up, but found it firmly rooted: it was not a pebble after all—but a plant! As he walked on, he saw others, dispersed all across the desert. His gunnery sergeant, Navarre, who happened to be a lawyer based in the South African countryside, had been familiar with *Lithops* and explained that the little water that had come was enough to make the plant burst forth in the most brilliant displays of color.

Around 80 to 95 percent of a plant is composed of water, which tells you how much plants rely on it for their survival. While *Lithops* might not need much water, they still need the occasional sprinkle. All plants need moisture. Even *Syntrichia caninervis*, a moss growing in the desert with tiny, whisker-like fibers at its leaf tips, is designed to harvest fog and direct the droplets to the moss's leaves. Water helps plants maintain cellular activity, gives them their form in soft tissues, cools them, carries nutrients to them, guides oxygen to their roots, and so much more.

Epiphytic plants, like some *Tillandsia*—otherwise known as air plants—affix themselves to everything from trees to telephone wires instead of soil but still require atmospheric moisture to feed them foliarly. And what would seem to be a burden to most host plants actually is a benefit: trees with epiphytes enjoy cooler temperatures and up to 20 percent less evaporation compared to trees without—revealing that epiphytes are more friend than freeloader, acting as both a humidifier and air conditioner to the tree that hosts them.

Not only do some plants depend on each other for water but humans also rely on the hydration plants provide. After plants siphon water up through their root zone, they "exhale" it into the atmosphere through their leaves, which ultimately contributes 10 percent of the moisture in our atmosphere—a component of the Earth's circulatory system.

But in very dry times, plants make do. Though permanently affixed to land, a plant's roots actively patrol beneath the dark environs for the first sign of rain. In well-functioning ecosystems, certain plants exhibit something known as "hydraulic lift" during periods of drought, whereby roots pull up water from deep soil layers at night and distribute the water to shallower roots in the upper layers of the soil. This has been shown to not only promote growth in the plants doing the heavy lifting but also ameliorate the drought for their neighbors, thereby keeping the area stable and in working order. Most plants have even made friendly pacts with other soil organisms to gain an upper edge, by festooning their roots and root hairs with fungal mycorrhizae, to increase moisture and nutrient retention, or by housing nitrogen-fixing bacteria in their root nodules for increased uptake of nitrogen—one of the more limited nutrients in plant growth, which becomes more bioavailable for plants with the bacteria's help.

Water's physiological purpose

Water serves many important physiological purposes in a plant's life, including aiding growth and metabolism. Just as water on the earth serves as a mode of transportation (think rivers), so does water that moves through a plant, serving as a conduit from soil to sky and back again. As a result, plants are able to convert many of nature's inorganic elements, which they get from the soil, such as calcium and magnesium, to organic compounds, which we in turn eat as "nutrients" to nourish ourselves. (Leafy greens and legumes are loaded with calcium that is necessary for healthy bones; and nuts, seeds, and greens are good sources of magnesium, which is used in more than 300 biochemical reactions in our bodies.) In fact, about 80 percent of the molecules in a plant are transported into the plant via water, and the remaining 20 percent are made in the plant using those inorganic elements. This conversion from inorganic minerals to organic nutrients is made via water through the root and plant tissue, and it's all regulated by osmotic pressure, which also helps maintain a plant's turgidity and keeps a plant upright.

Plants both "breathe" and "sweat"

According to the fossil record, plants have had "pores"—otherwise known as *stomata*—for hundreds of millions of years. Stomata have a fundamental role in the control of two of the most important plant processes—photosynthesis and transpiration. Most stomata are found on leaves, but they can also be found in fruits, flowers, stems, and even roots, depending on the plant. "Albino" plants—oftentimes the ones bred for collectors—typically have nonfunctional stomata, so it's important if you're considering a variegated variety not to get one with too many white leaves, as white leaves compromise both photosynthesis and transpiration, and it'll be the green leaves in the plant that will sustain the plant. It's one of the principal reasons why you typically don't see many variegated mutants in the wild; they're simply not as fit.

Fully functioning stomata, on the other hand, allow for both the diffusion of carbon dioxide gas from the air and the release of oxygen. But they also allow for *transpiration*, or the process by which water is transferred from the plant through evaporation via the stomata; transpiring also cools the plant, much in the way sweating cools a human. However, in plants, at least 90 percent of the water loss occurs via transpiration. It's part of what can make a house filled with houseplants, like mine, more humid.

Some may ask what the purpose is of a plant losing so much water, especially as water is so precious to a plant's lifecycle. On a macro level, transpiration is an important part of the earth's water cycle and climate stability—and it maintains the appropriate conditions for a community of plants to survive as a whole. The exchange of water vapor between leaf and atmosphere is enough to affect local climate, and regional and global weather and climate patterns in turn. Individual plants within a forest ecosystem, for instance, are acting in unison to regulate their preferred conditions for survival. That's part of the reason why it's common practice indoors to group plants together to help build up humidity for more humid-loving varieties. Plants that are grouped together transpire together.

The importance of the results of transpiration to a natural ecosystem—and in turn its plants—can be summarized by observations made during a trip I took to the Caribbean island of Antigua in 2005. Historically, the tropical isle had a wetter climate, which makes sense, considering it once was one of the most forested islands in the Caribbean. But as the rain forests were cleared to plant sugarcane during the colonial period, the climate became hotter and drier, and it rarely ever rained the way that it had prior to the clearing of the forests.

The reality is that plants create the environment they want to live in. The great Amazonian forest releases water into the air and brings that water back down to earth as rainfall, in order to maintain the appropriate climatic conditions for that forest. The hydraulic lifting of tree roots also waters the other plants around them, creating a stable environment. Cut a chunk of the forest down and that water cycle is broken—not just affecting the forest but also potentially causing drought in other areas of the world, as seen in places like São Paulo and the southern United States, for instance. According to a report released by Antonio Nobre, a researcher in Brazil's Earth System Science Center and foremost expert on Amazonian climate models, a reduction of 40 percent of the Amazon rain forest could trigger the area to transition to savannah—eventually eliminating intact forests that have not been felled.

Great forests are not the only collections of plants that help control macro- and microclimates. Even a microcosm of mosses on a wooded path is able to slow airflow in order to maintain the necessary moisture to keep it springy and green. Life will work to perpetuate itself in some of the most glorious ways. And more often than not, that life is working in unison with others of its kind—and not of its kind—to continue its existence.

Knowing that plants can change local climate conditions to better suit their needs demonstrates the powerful ways plants create our environments, and how we affect those environments for our plants, and inevitably ourselves. Perhaps we can take a lesson from our seemingly "passive"—yet incredibly proactive—green friends: we too create the community and the world that we want to live in, through our energy, attitude, and everyday actions.

Understanding how and why plants operate in this manner can help you obtain deeper knowledge and a stronger relationship with your plants, as you'll be able to begin to deduce what they need from you—and see how they adapt to their environment (like a chilly northern exposure), or why they can't.

Plants and soil

Perhaps there is no better example of living partnerships than there is between a plant's roots and the living soil it exists in. Soil serves many purposes and is often used to protect a plant's patrolling roots; keep a plant anchored and upright; provide a nutritious medium; help convey air and water to a plant's roots; and provide a rich ecosystem for it to thrive in, equipped with everything from microbes to mycelia.

When we think of soil, we often don't get the sense that it's alive, but it is in fact teeming with life—much of which remains hidden from our view. Given that most of us don't have a fancy electron microscope on hand to explore the depths of good dirt, the "I'll believe it when I see it" model might not cut it. Microscopic bacteria, archaea, fungi, nematodes, and protozoa all abound in a healthy soil substrate.

Even a mere teaspoon (about 4 grams) of healthy soil in a forested area may contain anywhere from 100 million to 1 billion bacteria, which are integral to both carbon and nitrogen recycling. In that same teaspoon of soil, there may also be 1 to 40 miles (1.6 to 64 kilometers) of fungal hyphae, hundreds of thousands of protozoa, and hundreds of nematodes, not to mention nutrients and leaf matter. All of this helps contribute to the health of the plant and its seedlings. Bacteria and archaea can help release nutrients for the plant; mycorrhizal fungi can also increase nutrient uptake, provide resistance against pathogens, and help reduce overall stress. Additionally, air pollutants and other volatile organic compounds (VOCs) like benzene and formaldehyde can be siphoned through a plant and rendered harmless in the rhizosphere, otherwise known as the root-soil interface. Additionally, roots—though operating in the dark belowground—are constantly moving and communicating. It's been shown that they can emit their own VOCs as a way to defend a plant against pathogens—further offering protection to the plant's overall health.

When we grow plants in planters, however, we remove them from this rich environment. And if we were to take soil from outside and put it in planters, it would react in a very different way in an enclosed environment—perhaps even harming the plant. So, instead, we often need to use sterile potting mixes and then build the soil up by perhaps adding beneficial microbes, mycorrhizae, and nutrients and even aerating the potting mix as it ages. Providing plants with well-draining potting mix is particularly important as it ensures the roots remain oxygenated.

THERE ARE, of course, so many other elements that we can discuss that can benefit plants, including temperature and airflow (both of which are more fully discussed in my Houseplant Masterclass on-line), but if you keep these three fundamentals of light, water, and soil in mind, then you'll be equipped to reevaluate the role you play in plants' lives. If you have yet to get a plant for your home, then the next step is getting the one that is right for you and your conditions. Keep the above information in mind as you choose and then make a home for your plants—watch how they react to the space you put them in and think about what they might need that they aren't getting, or even if they're getting too much of something, like if the soil is holding too much water and asphyxiating the roots.

One simple way to get good at plant observations is to designate one day per week solely to your plants. I've found that it's soul-lifting and life-affirming—so it's as good for me as it is for my plants. That's my Sunday—a day I really look forward to. Though I take care of my plants on the other days of the week—often walking through the house in the morning to top off anyone who needs water, deadheading any dried flowers, or picking off any dried leaves—I've found that having that one day devoted to my green friends makes caretaking less a quotidian chore and more of an activity to enjoy. It also helps me keep track of and observe positive or negative changes in my plants. Every day I learn from my plants; and much of what I've learned over the years is now being passed on to you. So go forth and plant.

GET-GROWING EXERCISE: LIGHT, PROJECTION, AND PLACEMENT

1. **Find the light.** What direction do your windows face? If you're not certain, take notice of where the sun rises and sets. If you still need help, most smartphones have a compass app, which can help determine the precise orientation of your windows. At what time does light enter your home? Perhaps you get soft morning light. Or hot afternoon light. How long does the light shine in your house? And does the light intensity change seasonally, if at all? Once you determine the direction, quality, and quantity of light that enters your home, begin to research what plants thrive best in those conditions.

2. **Observe a plant and guess its needs.** Next time you're in a plant shop, stop in and take a good look at the plants. Choose one in particular and see if you can intuit where that plant is from and what kind of climate or conditions it grows in. Are its leaves thin and tapered? Fat and succulent? Are they green and glossy or gray and fuzzy? Does it have thick roots, a bulb, or perhaps thin, webby roots? All of these characteristics can be used to intuit more about the plant, and can help you become more sensitive to a plant's care.

3. **Make the plant cozy.** Once you've determined which plant is most appropriate for your home, place it where

you think it'll do best. Observe it over the course of two weeks. How does it react to where it is placed? Does its stem move toward the window light? Are its leaves getting bigger? If it's not responding well, try to place it in another area, and observe how it reacts there. Sometimes finding the best location for a plant takes time and involves a little trial and error.

For those of us who are new to plants, I understand that you may need a bit of initial guidance in identifying the right ones for your home and lifestyle. Consider this chart a general guide to put you on a surer path:

I have a very sunny windowsill ➞ I'm hands-off when it comes to plants ➞ Cacti and most succulents [e.g., *Opuntia*, *Mammillaria*, *Astrophytum*, *Echeveria*]

I have a very sunny windowsill ➞ I'm attentive when it comes to plants ➞ Herbs and certain flowering plants [e.g., *Ocimum*, *Rosmarinus*, *Mentha*, *Pelargonium*]

I have some direct sunlight ➞ I can accommodate a larger plant ➞ *Ficus elastica*, *Ficus lyrata*

I have some direct sunlight ➞ I can accommodate a medium-size plant ➞ *Sansevieria* [*Dracaena*] or *Dracaena*

I have some direct sunlight ➞ I can accommodate a hanging plant ➞ *Tradescantia*

I have some direct sunlight ➝ I can accommodate a small plant ➝ *Saintpaulia*

I have a bright but relatively sunless window ➝ I can accommodate a larger plant ➝ *Monstera deliciosa* or *Schefflera*

I have a bright but relatively sunless window ➝ I can accommodate a medium-size plant ➝ **bromeliad** or *Spathiphyllum*

I have a bright but relatively sunless window ➝ I can accommodate a hanging plant ➝ *Scindapsus* or *Epipremnum* or *Philodendron*

I have a bright but relatively sunless window ➝ I can accommodate a small plant ➝ *Peperomia*

I have indirect light/a sunless window ➝ I'm hands-off when it comes to plants ➝ *Aglaonema* or *Aspidistra*

I have indirect light/a sunless window ➝ I'm attentive when it comes to plants ➝ *Adiantum, Asplenium* (or other ferns), or *Maranta*

CULTIVATING YOUR
PERSONAL GREEN SPACE

To forget how to dig the earth and tend
the soil is to forget ourselves.

—*Mahatma Gandhi*

Those who contemplate the beauty of the earth
find reserves of strength that will endure as long as life lasts.
There is something infinitely healing in the repeated refrains
of nature—the assurance that dawn comes after night,
and spring after winter.

—*Rachel Carson*

· · · · · · · · · ·

*"Somehow, taking time to nurture my plants, especially
in the winter months, is a method of self-care. Without
my plants my house wouldn't be my home." —Rachael*

When I shared my apartment in Williamsburg with a roommate over ten years ago, there were very few plants in the house. To be honest, I didn't even know how long I would stay in the city when I first moved here, so getting plants didn't seem in the cards, so to speak.

Now, fourteen years later, I have managed to grow roots in Brooklyn, having hollowed out a beautiful, old postwar apartment in a former steel building and formed a tight-knit community of friends. If you follow me on Instagram or watch my YouTube videos, or if you've taken the Masterclass or workshops I teach, you'll have seen that my home is filled with plant life; you might think it looks beautiful or at least peaceful—and you might worry you'll not be able to create a sanctuary of your own. But I want to reassure you that my home hasn't always looked as it does now. It was over time—through following my own intuition and interests, and much trial and error—that my home in the city eventually became my little oasis of green.

When I first lived alone, it took me many months to break the habit of keeping to myself in my room most of the time. But after a while, I began to walk around the house with greater surety, probing different rooms, wiping the dust from the windowsills with my fingertip, and even moving furniture. I wanted the space to open up, so I pushed the beds to the corners and removed the coffee table and second desk. I got rid of the clunky television from the nineties that had sat enshrouded behind a Japanese blind, which I kept—it became the perfect trellis for a clambering *Epipremnum aureum*, or golden pothos. Each change was incremental and happened when I was ready.

These incremental changes emerged as I started to cultivate habits and rituals, which I'll discuss in depth in this chapter. It's tempting to jump on trends and suddenly identify as a "plant person," a "devout vegan," or a member of the "zero-waste brigade" in order to feel mindful. All of these things can be good, but a healthy, peaceful mind-set actually starts with something subtler and intangible, yet far more potent: a more observant way of being. For me, plants and the rituals I've created around them have helped me contribute thoughtfully to my surrounding environment—and find solace in a city that doesn't encourage slowing down.

Organizing my life around nature has, no pun intended, helped me feel grounded as the world around me has been uprooted. Until a few years ago, my home was surrounded by a vintage furniture restoration shop, two woodworking facilities, and a more modern-day steel-working facility. Now a sports bar, a swanky coffee shop, a dentist's office, and a plant shop have moved in—in that order. Though the surrounding environment, and even its tempo, has changed since my move, my daily rituals with my plants have remained the same, giving me a solid sense of home.

My apartment, where I house my plants, is far from perfect—the plumbing doesn't work well, the windows are hard to open and close, and I'm positive there is no insulation, given the way the drafts of cold wind in winter fill the rooms with assured, icy tenacity. But this is my own personal green space, bringing me the spiritual and emotional clarity that I take with me everywhere I go. In this chapter, you'll learn how to start building your own.

Your garden as ritual

Though heavily influenced by traditional Chinese gardens, Japanese gardening became its own distinct style, inspired by the topography and natural landscapes of the country. The *Sakuteiki*, published in the eleventh century, is the earliest known treatise on gardening and is still relevant to garden designers today. The flow or asymmetry of the garden, the discipline in setting the stones, the types of artifacts, and the way a path progressed or halted, for example, are replete with symbolism, thought, and meaning. We may inattentively walk through a Japanese garden because we are not enculturated to understand its layers of meaning, perhaps noticing only an interesting pine or a blooming lotus flower, but oftentimes the designer of such gardens has intended the design to provoke deep reflection and thought for those who walk through it.

The tea garden, for instance, is steeped in symbolism. Paths to tea houses are often interpretations of the routes that pilgrims took through the mountainsides, and the plants picked to adorn the gardens were chosen to reflect as much. Gateways or doorways to the tea room were often lowered so one entering would need to stoop, which was an act of humility, symbolizing that the material world was being left behind and that a time of introspection, contemplation, and higher consciousness was called for. Finding ceremony and the celebration in life's little moments resonates deeply. This understanding is the key to a more fulfilled existence, even if what we have is very little.

I use Sunday for this exact purpose. Sunday is my chosen "holy day"; it's the day that I fully devote to my plants—potting, watering, propagating, and doing all of the other delightful chores of plant care. I don't like to be rushed, as it's time for conscientiousness and observation; it's the main reason why I rarely book meetings for that day.

For me, Sunday is a "moving meditation," which should be free of any fettered thoughts or preoccupations. This ritual allows me to enjoy the spiritual, emotional, and physical benefits of plant care. The great Japanese Zen Buddhist monk Hakuin Ekaku said, "Meditation in the midst of activity was far better than meditation in stillness," and I have found this to be true for me, particularly when it comes to my plants, as have many people in the plant community:

> "During times of stress, I've found that when I take the time to give attention to and tend to each plant's needs, to appreciate any new growth in every plant, I feel a tangible sense of relaxation and calm. When I sit on my living room floor, having my mini jungle in front of me is such a comfort—a distraction I never get tired of looking at. I've only recently gained an outdoor space for gardening, but the physical labor of tending to a garden or yard has a similar meditative and calming effect. It's so satisfying." —Jessica

"When I am caring for my plants I feel serene and calm. It is like a ritual or a meditation that gives me pause and deep relaxation. I can't imagine living without them now."
—Sarah A. @clandestine_thylacine

"I recently have faced an unexpected health issue and personal loss that has been challenging to deal with. I pulled myself up off of the couch to water my houseplants. This was a small step, but I recall the small sense of accomplishment I felt afterwards. With that small encouragement, I took a moment to take myself out of hibernation again and go outside to get the mail from the mailbox. On the way there, I noticed my aromatic asters and pink muhly grass were blooming. When I went closer to look, five monarch butterflies fluttered around me, and I realized that it was the start of the monarch migration season. More and more, I went outside to see how many butterflies were there and if I could take photos of them. Along the way, I would notice a weed or two and pull them. An hour later, I'm still outside and notice a hummingbird fluttering around my *Salvia*. The mindfulness that being in the garden cultivated within me has helped me as I heal. Gardening is a grounding activity and helped me to feel more in the moment and centered in my body." —Susan Morgan

"I am a classical musician, so I spend a lot of time indoors practicing. . . . Plants help me create a calm atmosphere and help me stay focused. I actually move some plants in front

of where I sit when I practice so I'm not tempted to get up
and do other things." —Marissa Takaki

I didn't begin to form routines around my plants until after my
roommate moved out of our apartment. When she did, I sold off
most of our furniture and my apartment was suddenly barren, so
barren that when I spoke loudly enough, a resonant echo would reverberate off the exposed brick walls. I wanted a plant that was big
enough to fill the space—but not so big that I wouldn't be able to
lug it upstairs, as most old lofts don't have elevators.

I purchased my first plant from my local plant shop, Sprout
Home. It was a *Ficus lyrata*, or fiddle-leaf fig, a species which is
originally from western African, lowland tropical rain forests, but
now has become the iconic, statuesque, big-leaved tree that you so
often see in the lobbies of the glass-walled high-rises that have begun to populate my neighborhood.

I placed the fig between two southwest-facing windows—in
what was then my bedroom, but what has now become my work
room. It was perfect. The sunlight shone through the leaves, producing a most glorious gold-green frondescence that felt both familiar and mystical. As with any plant I get, I didn't just place it in
the room and go about my business. I tend to hang on to the feeling
for the moment and stand in admiration of the other living, breathing being that's now within my presence. After all, it's there to be
admired, and cared for, so that in turn it cares for you—cleaning
your air, calming your mind, and literally tapping into your ancient,
biological need to feel connected to nature.

The latter point is an important one, and perhaps the very reason
I started my plant-based ventures and authored this book. Those of

us who have chosen to live in cities, surrounded by four walls and concrete sidewalks and asphalt streets, are likely the most in need of our own little oasis of green—outside, in our homes, and in our hearts. Going back to Tama's idea of "prisoner-of-war plants," I would argue that if anything, we've made ourselves prisoners—far away from our Garden of Eden. I do not have to spew the latest research to assure you of this, because you feel it; and I see it when people walk into my home. There's something about the quiet, searching, and persistent nature of plants that brings us immeasurable joy on the deepest of levels. Even if it's not a scorching-hot day, most people would prefer to walk on a tree-lined street than one that is devoid of plant life. We gravitate toward it because it's beautiful, it's peaceful, it's energizing.

I DON'T REMEMBER my second houseplant. I don't think it matters so much any longer. An indoor ecosystem of sorts has emerged since I bought my first—an outward manifestation, no doubt, of my desire to be close to nature while doing what I love in the "urban jungle." I've often said that the only way that I've survived in this city for so long is by bringing nature indoors and developing a ritual around my plants. And now my plants have made these four walls very much their home, as I have. They have, quite literally, put down roots—and so have I.

When my home and its now-fecund greenery went viral in the summer of 2016, it very much came as a surprise to me. Sure, plants are cool and are experiencing their moment "in the spotlight"— and of course, the sheer number of plants had something to do with it (I have around 550 species and 200 varieties of plants and well over 1,000 individual specimens now), but many people's fascination with my space was really about something much larger.

Reading people's questions online; opening up my home for meditators and tours; ushering volunteers and passersby through our community gardens; giving public, private, and online plant workshops; and embarking on running a plant-related business, I've begun to ask larger questions: Why are people fascinated by all these plants?

> "I suffer from seasonal depression as well as anxiety. . . . I read that plants, candles, and soft, organic textures are all easy ways to create a sense of warmth, or *hygge*, if you will, in your home. I started collecting plants and tending to the ones I already had better. I started reading about plant care, and for me not only did [plants] help me feel better from an aesthetic point of view, but I also found that taking care of them was enjoyable for me; it made me feel as if I was accomplishing something in seeing them thrive." —Katey

> "Taking care of plants gives me a sense of satisfaction. It's wonderful watching them grow, learning what they do and don't like. When I walk in my room and see my plants, my heart flutters a little. They are all my children."
> —Alexis Ortiz

> "I don't live in the greatest of apartments, so I decided to make it more 'livable.' The first thing I did was get a few plants and I was amazed at how [they] livened up the place! Now I have as many plants as I can fit. It's what I think

I needed all along—something that could make me feel
safe, warm, and homey." —Julius R.

Sure, a part of it has to do with the seemingly uncanny ability to
keep a plant alive—let alone hundreds of plants—but that's just the
superficial wonderment. What underlies the fascination is how my
plants create a unique sense of place and of home. People connect
with the idea that caring for plants is about nurturing yourself, by
creating the environment that you want to live in—both inside and
outside the home—and that is by far one of the greatest lessons
plants can teach us.

Nature inspire artfulness

My plants greet me every morning as I wake up. This makes it hard
not to think of them, as they are always present. They have become
such a fixture of my apartment that they may as well be an out-
growth of the walls and other furnishings. I suppose it's why I elevate my plants to the status of "living art."

No one doubts Mother Nature's beauty. We intuit the beauty of
order and sequence in fiddleheads, pinecones, and sunflowers,
even if we cannot explain why they are beautiful. For this reason,
nature has inspired great art since the beginning of human culture,
from the depictions of plants from ancient Mesopotamia and Egypt
to the Hudson River School painters. The writings in the *Sakuteiki*, the eleventh-century Japanese text on gardening, even suggest: "Visualize the famous landscapes of our country and come to

understand their most interesting points. Recreate the essence of these scenes in the garden, but do so interpretively, not strictly." The writing instructs us to be inspired by nature, to plant as she would, but not take her so literally. In the process, the human interpretation becomes the art. Luckily for us, plants make it easy to see beauty.

And is not my very home a domesticated imitation of nature? I think of it as a sort of artistic attempt to showcase what nature herself might look like if she grew inside a box that was crafted with brick, glass, and cement, tended by human hands. But unlike most paintings and sculpture, my apartment's verdant life is ever-changing. And on the flip side, doesn't being in the very presence of nature inspire creation—therefore giving birth to replicas and reflections of her? Nature's palpable puissant yet quiet energy brings upon such creativity—even in quantifiable terms, as exemplified by science—that it is undeniable that we humans are in touch with a subconscious force that is ever present but not always acknowledged. We pass our creations off as "discoveries" and "inventions," but they are merely our interpretations and attempts to re-create what we inherently already know as "perfect."

Surrounding yourself with the beauty of nature will surely bring you a sense of calm. About four times a year, I offer up my home for people in the city to come and meditate. First-timers will often marvel at the magnitude of plants, standing agape at the entrance as they stumble out of their shoes. Most often people leave my space with a newfound appreciation and desire to bring plants into their lives. The mise-en-scène at my home is not overwhelming, as each plant feels very much "in its place," but it is awe-inspiring. A large *Monstera deliciosa* clambers up a mossy beam; an *Epipremnum au-*

reum cascades around a full-length mirror, only to scamper up the other side. A set of philodendrons and pothos of various species wend and wind their way around a hardwood pillar; and a *Hedera helix* has taken up residence in every crack or crevice that it can fit its coarse, brush-like rootlets into. The plants have clearly made this their home, as much as I have made it mine; and I'm happy—in some small way—to share that with others.

Plants are inherently peaceful creatures—or perhaps their very nature inspires peace. If you have plants in your home, then you likely already recognize this; and fellow plant owners wouldn't be amazed to know that there is substantial evidence that indoor plants bring comfort, calm, and even creativity to those in their presence. This brings forth a well-founded theory, popularized by biologist E. O. Wilson, that there is an innate inclination for people to associate with nature, which has been termed *biophilia*. In sum, we want to be around plants; we know, deep down, that they make us feel at home. For all of us who choose to live with plants, it's a way to return to our metaphorical and spiritual Garden of Eden.

Nature inspires togetherness

"Your name is Summer Rayne," an Uber driver once said to me. I couldn't discern whether it was a question or an affirmation. His eyes wistfully trailed off into the distance, and then glistened as he looked up to meet my gaze in the mirror.

"Yes. You say it with such passion!" I noted.

"Well," he said, turning over his right shoulder with a smile, "in

India, where my family is from, we always celebrate the first summer rain. It has a special smell—a sweet, earthy smell."

I know well the fragrance that he so longingly spoke of.

Though I had never traveled to India for the first summer rain, I grew up in bucolic northeastern Pennsylvania. Penn's Woods, as it has been named, is an appropriate part of the country to grow up for a plant-interested kid, as the state is abundant with plant life and has a unique geologic history. I loved walking through the woods behind my house; the first thaw would bring spring ephemerals, like trout lilies (*Erythronium americanum*), whose striking saffron bonnets hung like shooting stars on stems that sprung forth from mottled russet-green leaves that mimicked the dappled light on the forest floor. Lime-green, tumescent buds on trees, waxed and polished to a military shine, would signal the official appearance of spring.

But dew-drenched autumn days were my favorite. That's when a forest was the most feracious with the humic ambrosia of the earth's ample bosom. The flowers of witch hazel (*Hamamelis virginiana*), which seemed to be tied like tattered yellow ribbons to scraggy, bare stems, filled the air with their demure fragrance; layers of fallen leaves, sodden from the previous night's hibernal lament, would stick to the soles of my well-worn moccasins; and the scent of deep, rich humus would rise up—an arpeggio of terrene perfume—sating my lungs.

The smell of wet earth is as complex and as varied as that of fine wine to a master sommelier, but its underlying essence is unmistakable. Strangely enough, I was reunited with the smell not in the forest but on a visit to a perfumer in Cape Town. Tammy Frazer of Frazer Parfum had asked me what my most favorite smell was in the world. I described my seasonal walks in the woods. She shuffled briefly behind her counter and lifted a small glass vial from her drawer. "It's *geosmin*," she told me.

"Not the most romantic name," I thought, but I took a good whiff. That was it: a Pennsylvania walk in the woods in a bottle. It turns out that *geosmin* is not endemic to my woods. Its name is derived from the Greek language, literally "earth smell," and it is a ubiquitous compound that is produced not by the soil itself, but by the microbes, algae, and fungi living in it or in nearby aquatic environments. Actinobacteria and myxobacteria seem to be the most prevalent in soil. During the dry season, the microbes spread myxospores, the equivalent to spores in ferns, which can hitch a ride easily, whether it be by wind, foot, feather, or fur. What's miraculous, however, is as soon as the rain quenches the parched fauces of terra firma, the earth becomes gravid with the loamy afterbirth of microbial life. The myxobacteria, which feed on decaying matter, can actually "swarm" on the soil's surface like an encroaching filmy slime; and the actinobacteria grow extensive mycelia, similar to fungi, and often live symbiotically with plant roots in a similar manner to fungi, fixing nitrogen for the small price of some of the plant's sugars: a true neighborly exchange!

It's these microbes that impart the earthy flavor to beets, mushrooms, carp, and clams. They also provide a plethora of antibiotics for human and animal health—as well as serve as the basis for many insecticides and pesticides, given that their very nature protects and aids plants. And they have been found everywhere throughout the Earth—from ice-bound Antarctica to the tropics, from sea level to the highest mountain peaks, and in the densest tropical rain forests and even dust-blown deserts. That's how this "earth smell" has become the characteristic scent after a rain throughout the world. And though some of us are more sensitive to the smell than others, the average person can detect as little as 0.7 parts per billion of geosmin. So minute an amount can trigger such a stimulation of senses and an upwelling of primal memory that it's been hypothesized that the odor helped guide our earliest ancestors to the nearest source of food after extended periods of drought.

Though my taxi driver and I had grown up 8,000 miles (12,874.8 kilometers) away from one another, we had both delighted in a shared experience, as ordinary and yet strangely complex as the smell of soil. Rare is the occasion that I go on forest walks in the city to reunite with my childhood rambles; and after parting ways with my cabbie, I wondered if he had smelled fresh earth since departing his home country.

Experiences such as this can forge unexpected fraternity with other human beings, if you're open to the connection. Of course, it would be easy for us to adorn our homes with plants and call it a day, but given our social nature, many of us want to share these experiences with others. Social networks have become an active place to share stories and become inspired by others, but I've always found it hard to develop deep connections through social media because the interactions exist strictly on one's mobile device or desktop.

One day I had wanted to see if the people who followed me and whom I followed on Instagram had an interest in getting together. I put out a post to see if anyone would be interested in participating in a plant swap, which is an event that would involve trading plants. Much to my amazement, at least fifty people responded, and thus started a series of swaps—and not only in New York. Those swaps inspired others to organize similar events around the world. Plant swaps are incredible ways to bring people together, and can be as low-key or as formal as you want to make them. The rules were kept pretty simple: bring a good spirit and at least one pest-free plant, potted or bare root, for trade. If you wanted to trade a plant, you would be required to speak with the person(s) that you were looking to trade with, and as a result, lots of connections and friendships were forged, which in turn gave more meaning and greater connectivity to the people on the other side of our mobile devices.

My community garden is another place that creates a space for people to come together. More like a patchwork quilt of participation and ideas, a community garden's charm is in the individual and collective contributions of those who participate in its growth and upkeep. Had it not been for my garden, I would have not had the pleasure of meeting most of the people in the community who garden there. Because of those connections, I've felt ever more encouraged to not just focus on my own garden plot but to help contribute to the garden as a whole. An important lesson I've learned, as I shared earlier, is that you create the community you want to live in:

"I found refuge in learning about plants—how to care for them, where they're from, how to propagate them. . . . Eventually, I discovered the Instagram plant community, made some local plant friends, and have truly found myself in plants. I love my job as a professor, but now I feel I have a true hobby that I am dedicated to, which I actually allow myself to spend time focusing on, and which removes me from the stress of academia. I can truly say that plants helped me recover from some trauma and find a way to move on into a new space in life with which I am happy!" —Sabrina

"I always liked plants, but what made me really express my love for them [even] more are all the people that I've met through the houseplant community, online and offline. I went to my first plant swap in October of 2017 and traded a few plants. When I look at how [the plants have] grown since then, I think of the people I traded them with."
—Sammy

"I have terrible high and low mood swings that hit without warning. Since bringing plants into my home I have felt an overwhelming feeling of peace for the first time in a long time. They make me happy, they give me a reason to get out of bed, and, most importantly, the plant community is one of the kindest communities I have ever been a part of."
—Ellie Lang

Once you've successfully invited plants into your own life, why not take it a step further and build—or join—a community of like-minded people? Doing so is just another way to fight the toxic loneliness of modern life indoors.

Plants inspire us to reach our fullest potential

While writing this book, I got a call from my friend and colleague Allan Schwarz, the architect and forest conservationist I spoke of earlier, who had discovered *Lithops* in the Namib Desert while on active duty. He doesn't call as often as he had before, but when he does, I know it's because he wants to talk about something important.

Allan is not someone who sits idly by while someone or something is in need. If you get him talking about his work long enough, you can see tears well up in his eyes. It's hard labor, very rewarding yet very thankless at the same time, and very, very much a part of him. He called me that day while I sat at my table writing, and he spoke of his troubles. As he talked, I heard the pride but hint of defeat in his voice; I knew, deep down, what he was feeling. "I won't bore you with the typical kleptocratic government bullshit," he started off. "But I have to have a deep think as to whether I can carry this on," he uttered with a little breath of incredulous disbelief. "I'm getting older, and I'm not sure how much—"

I cut him off because I didn't want to have him say what he felt obliged to say. I know giving in after twenty years of his life's work would feel equivalent to dismembering his arms, or giving up his firstborn. "Why don't you take the month of September to really have a long, hard think," I said. "Get your mind in order, and figure out realistically what is the most important, the most doable."

People like Allan are not one in a million—they're more like one in 100 million, or one in 500 million. He regrows trees in deforested regions to conserve and heal the land so the original species of that area can not only survive—but thrive. I've spent time with him, collecting seeds, planting seedlings, and pressing oils—but it's infinitesimal compared to the decades of work, tenderness, and tenacity that he's devoted to the land, its plants, and its people.

I would venture to say that each one of us who has picked up or has been gifted this book has the care and love that Allan has for plants and the ecosystems from which they come. We don't always have the capacity or frame of mind to do work like Allan, or even have the ability or chance to see some of these ecosystems about which I write, but we should begin to recognize that we all have a place to make positive changes—in our lives and the lives of others—no matter our role, especially now that we know so much more about what plants have to teach us! There may not be as many Allans in this world—those who have devoted their lives to conserving so many of the plants we love, and have yet to love—and there may not be that many growers, but what I do know is that there are plenty of plant lovers—and yet-to-be plant lovers. And each one of us can make positive changes—individually and collectively— together!

Nature gives us a true gift—and rarely asks for anything in return other than that we take care of her in times of need. All the houseplants in the world will never supplant nature. They can, however, share in their origin story of how they get to our homes, pique our curiosity—acting as a lens into the greater world beyond the garden center—and maybe even, in their quiet, unassuming ways, encourage us to become better stewards here on Earth. That's one of the very important lessons that I've learned from my plants. It's why I encourage people to see that it's not about just surrounding yourself with green in your own homes but getting out into your community and the greater world to make a difference. If anything, plants give us a sense of peace, a sense of place, and if we're to consider this world—beyond our four walls—our home, then I can't think of any place better to start than caring for a plant.

ACKNOWLEDGMENTS

No book is ever done in isolation, and *How to Make a Plant Love You* is no exception. A big thank-you goes out to Tony Gardner, my dear friend and literary agent; you not only go to bat for me every time, but you also always take precious time out of your day to lend an ear when I need to talk. "All a part of the service," you say, but you know you always go above and beyond. Working with you alone makes me want to write more books!

To my fellow author Starre Vartan, who was there to help early on. Oftentimes an author can get too into her own work, so I am forever grateful that you took the time to serve as both a sounding board and a critical eye. A big high five to illustrator Mark Conlan. I reached out years ago because I loved your work and am so grateful you chose to illustrate my book (and the Houseplant Masterclass) with me. Your creative talents provide so much energy to the pages!

A wholehearted thank-you to Sander van Dijk—partner, creative counterpart, and friend. You have put up with a lot of plant talk—and facilitate my passion in so many ways! Your kindness, generosity, and support over the years have been boundless and I will forever be indebted. To Damon Horowitz, who had encouraged me to start Homestead Brooklyn from the start—this book probably wouldn't have ever materialized if it weren't for your initial suggestion. And to my other best friend and creative counterpart, Joey L., who has become like family in this big city that we call home.

To the Optimism Team: Friend and compatriot Simon Sinek, who would have thought a chance meeting in a taxi cab line would transpire into friendship and working together?! You have been nothing but supportive through the entire time we've known one another. Thank you for not only believing in me—but also bringing this book concept to life under your imprint. And to the rest of the team: My editor Leah Trouwborst, who encouraged me to think bigger and do better with the book—and yet was incredibly open-minded to all of my suggestions. Toni Sciarra Poynter: I am forever grateful that you decided to come on board. You took the time to listen to my thoughts and were able to help synthesize some of the most sensitive and salient aspects to help shape the book into what it is today. And Adrian Zackheim, Helen Healey, Christopher Sergio, Madeline Montgomery, Marisol Salaman, Tara Gilbride, Olivia Peluso, Jean Hartig, Sally Knapp, Meredith Clark, Gabriel Levinson, the Start with Why crew, and anyone else whom I have yet to meet or may have left out: thank you!

Special gratitude goes out to all the people whom I interviewed for this book, including those who didn't inevitably make it into the book. Some of those include: Peter Fraissinet, William L. Crepet, Anna Stalter, Lawrence McCrea, Chad Husby, Chad Davis, Munther Younes, Bruce Bugbee, Richard Lenat, Steve Rosenbaum, and Bob Hoffbauer. And to my professors and mentors over the years: Ernie Keller, Chet Kowalsky, the late Tom Eisner, Barbara Bedford, Ellen Harrison, Tom Gavin, Bobbi Peckarsky, Allan Schwarz, Wade Davis, Martin von Hildebrand, and many others. And a big bout of gratitude goes out to all of the people from all around the world who were open and vulnerable enough to share their precious personal stories with me for this book. I hope you see the value that you've brought—not only to the text, but also to others who read *How to Make a Plant Love You.*

To my readers or listeners (in the case of the audiobook): thank you for supporting what I've written. I hope it provides you much joy and inspiration; and I invite you to learn more about the beautiful world of plants through my other channels, on YouTube, Instagram, Facebook, and my websites homesteadbrooklyn.com and houseplantmasterclass.com.

And last and certainly not the least, to my family: my parents, Bob and Diane; my grandparents, Smittie and Lil; and my brother, Travis. Thanks for celebrating my weirdness.

RESOURCES

For further resources by Summer Rayne Oakes you can visit:

HOMESTEAD BROOKLYN

homesteadbrooklyn.com

A photo-based blog featuring gardening insights, home-cooked recipes, and more.

PLANT ONE ON ME

youtube.com/user/summerrayneoakes

A YouTube series documenting indoor and outdoor gardening tips, plant-care advice, botanical excursions, and behind-the-scenes tours with botanical gardens, greenhouses, and growers.

HOUSEPLANT MASTERCLASS

houseplantmasterclass.com

A comprehensive audio-visual online course to teach you how to care for houseplants.

INSTAGRAM

@homesteadbrooklyn

An Instagram account showcasing daily plant and gardening inspiration and insights.

NOTES

CHAPTER 1: THE MASS MIGRATION

16 **In the United States:** Lamber, Lisa. "More Americans move to cities in past decade-Census." Reuters, March 26, 2012. https://reuters.com /article/usa-cities-population/more-americans-move-to-cities-in -past-decade-census-idUSL2E8EQ5AJ20120326.

16 **And of the general:** "Millennials Prefer Cities to Suburbs, Subways to Driveways." Nielsen, March 4, 2014. http://nielsen.com/us/en/insights /news/2014/millennials-prefer-cities-to-suburbs-subways-to-driveways .html.

16 **And today, 55 percent:** "68% of the world population projected to live in urban areas by 2050, says UN." United Nations Department of Economic and Social Affairs, May 16, 2018. https://un.org/development/desa/en /news/population/2018-revision-of-world-urbanization-prospects.html.

18 **A 2016 Gallup poll:** Nelson, Bailey, and Brandon Rigoni. "Few Millennials Are Engaged at Work." Gallup, January 23, 2019. https://news .gallup.com/businessjournal/195209/few-millennials-engaged-work .aspx.

18 **A large-scale 2016 study:** Primack, Brian A., Ariel Shensa, César G. Escobar-Viera, Erica L. Barrett, Jaime E. Sidani, Jason B. Colditz, and A. Everette James. "Use of multiple social media platforms and symptoms of depression and anxiety: A nationally-representative study among US young adults." *Computers in Human Behavior* 69 (2017): 1–9.

19 **And about 67 percent:** Calfas, Jennifer. "Millennials Spend a Big Part of Their Work Day Stressed Out By Their Finances," *Money*, June 1, 2017. http://time.com/money/4794497/millennials-finances-money-stressed -work.

19 **A 2014 Gallup poll:** Dugan, Andrew, and Stephanie Marken. "Student Debt Linked to Worse Health and Less Wealth." Gallup, August 7, 2014. http://news.gallup.com/poll/174317/student-debt-linked-worse-health -less-wealth.aspx.

20 **According to the 2016 National Gardening Survey:** Garden Research. National Gardening Survey 2016 Edition.

CHAPTER 2: OUR NEED FOR NATURE

29 **This, along with the Republic's:** Tan, Audrey. "Not a concrete jungle: Singapore beats 16 cities in urban green areas." *Straits Times*, February 23, 2017. https://straitstimes.com/singapore/environment/not-a-concrete -jungle-singapore-beats-16-cities-in-green-urban-areas.

30 **During certain times:** "Urban Heat Island in Singapore." Cooling Singapore, January 23, 2019. https://www.coolingsingapore.sg /uhi-singapore.

31 **Through its greening efforts:** "Urban Heat Island in Singapore." Cooling Singapore, January 23, 2019. https://www.coolingsingapore.sg /uhi-singapore.

34 **Today, about a third:** Ministry of the Environment and Water Resources Ministry of National Development. *Sustainable Singapore Blueprint 2015: Our Home, Our Environment, Our Future*. 2015. https://sustainable development.un.org/content/documents/16253Sustainable_Singapore _Blueprint_2015.pdf.

35 **One study found:** South, Eugenia C., Bernadette C. Hohl, Michelle C. Kondo, John M. MacDonald, and Charles C. Branas. "Effect of greening vacant land on mental health of community-dwelling adults: A cluster

randomized trial." *JAMA Network Open* 1, no. 3 (2018): e180298-e180298. https://jamanetwork.com/journals/jamanetworkopen/fullarticle /2688343.

35 **Even if you can't walk:** Chang, Chen-Yen, and Ping-Kun Chen. "Human response to window views and indoor plants in the workplace." *HortScience* 40, no. 5 (2005): 1354–59.

35 **Those fortunate enough:** Ulrich, Roger S. "View through a window may influence recovery from surgery." *Science* 224, no. 4647 (1984): 420–21.

35 **This calming effect:** Lee, Min-sun, Juyoung Lee, Bum-Jin Park, and Yoshifumi Miyazaki. "Interaction with indoor plants may reduce psychological and physiological stress by suppressing autonomic nervous system activity in young adults: a randomized crossover study." *Journal of Physiological Anthropology* 34, no. 1 (2015): 21.

36 **It was found:** Wichrowski, Matthew J., Jonathan Whiteson, François Haas, Ana Mola, and Mariano J. Rey. "Effects of horticultural therapy on mood and heart rate in patients participating in an inpatient cardiopulmo-nary rehabilitation program." *Journal of Cardiopulmonary Rehabilitation and Prevention* 25, no. 5 (2005): 270–74.

39 **In Egypt:** Gerlach-Spriggs, Nancy, Richard Enoch Kaufman, and Sam Bass Warner Jr. *Restorative Gardens: The Healing Landscape.* New Haven, CT: Yale University Press, 2004.

39 **And in the 1800s:** Nightingale, Florence. *Notes on Nursing (Revised with Additions).* London: Ballière Tindall, 1996.

40 **People who were studied:** Park, Bum-Jin, Yuko Tsunetsugu, Tamami Kasetani, Takahide Kagawa, and Yoshifumi Miyazaki. "The physiological effects of Shinrin-yoku (taking in the forest atmosphere or forest bathing): evidence from field experiments in 24 forests across Japan." *Environmental Health and Preventive Medicine* 15, no. 1 (2010): 18; Lee, Juyoung, Bum-Jin Park, Yuko Tsunetsugu, Tatsuro Ohira, Takahide Kagawa, and Yoshifumi Miyazaki. "Effect of forest bathing on physiological and psychological responses in young Japanese male subjects." *Public Health* 125, no. 2 (2011): 93–100; Li, Qing, K. Morimoto, M. Kobayashi, H. Inagaki, M. Katsumata, Yukiyo Hirata, Kimiko Hirata, et al. "Visiting a forest, but not a city, increases human natural killer activity and expression of anti-cancer proteins." *International Journal of Immunopathol-*

ogy and Pharmacology 21, no. 1 (2008): 117–27; Li, Q., K. Morimoto, A. Nakadai, H. Inagaki, M. Katsumata, T. Shimizu, Y. Hirata, et al. "Forest bathing enhances human natural killer activity and expression of anti-cancer proteins." *International Journal of Immunopathology and Pharmacology* 20, no. S2 (2007): 3–8.

41 **The back yard:** Campbell, Helen. *Darkness and Daylight; Or, Lights and Shadows of New York Life: A Woman's Story of Gospel, Temperance, Mission, and Rescue Work*. Hartford, CT: A. D. Worthington & Company, 1892.

CHAPTER 3: WE ONLY LOVE WHAT WE NOTICE

50 **Yet eight of the ten:** Dugan, Frank M. "Shakespeare, plant blindness, and electronic media." *Plant Science Bulletin* 62, no. 2 (2016): 85–93.

52 **Though no control group:** Krosnick, Shawn E., Julie C. Baker, and Kelly R. Moore. "The Pet Plant Project: Treating Plant Blindness by Making Plants Personal." *The American Biology Teacher* 80, no. 5 (2018): 339–45.

CHAPTER 5: A HUMAN HISTORY OF HOUSEPLANTS

96 **As such, Tiberius enjoyed:** Dehgan, Bijan. *Public Garden Management: A Global Perspective*. Vol. 2. Xlibris Corporation, 2014.

96 **The first wooden greenhouse:** Dehgan, Bijan. *Public Garden Management: A Global Perspective*. Vol. 2. Xlibris Corporation, 2014.

105 **Nearly a third:** Biggs, Caroline. "Plant-Loving Millennials at Home and at Work," *New York Times*, March 9, 2018. https://nytimes.com /2018/03/09/realestate/plant-loving-millennials-at-home-and-at -work.html.

CHAPTER 6: GETTING TO KNOW YOUR PLANTS

116 **Plants are so attuned:** Gagliano, Monica, Mavra Grimonprez, Martial Depczynski, and Michael Renton. "Tuned in: plant roots use sound to locate water." *Oecologia* 184, no. 1 (2017): 151–60.

CHAPTER 7: HOW TO MAKE A PLANT LOVE YOU

134 **And what would seem:** Stuntz, Sabine, Ulrich Simon, and Gerhard Zotz. "Rainforest air-conditioning: the moderating influence of epiphytes on the microclimate in tropical tree crowns." *International Journal of Biometeorology* 46, no. 2 (2002): 53–59.

135 **This has been shown to not only:** Dawson, Todd E. "Hydraulic lift and water use by plants: implications for water balance, performance and plant-plant interactions." *Oecologia* 95, no. 4 (1993): 565–74.

138 **According to a report released:** Nobre, Antonio Donato. *The Future Climate of Amazonia, Scientific Assessment Report.* Translated by American Journal Experts, Margi Moss. São José dos Campos, Brazil: ARA, CCST-INPE, INPA, 2014.

140 **Even a mere teaspoon:** Hoorman, J. J. *The Role of Soil Bacteria.* Agriculture and Natural Resources Fact Sheet SAG: 13–11. Columbus, OH: Ohio State University, 2011.

140 **hundreds of thousands of protozoa:** Ingham, Elaine, Andrew R. Moldenke, and Clive Arthur Edwards. *Soil Biology Primer.* Soil and Water Conservation Society, 2000.

140 **All of this helps:** Mendes, Rodrigo, Paolina Garbeva, and Jos M. Raaijmakers. "The rhizosphere microbiome: significance of plant beneficial, plant pathogenic, and human pathogenic microorganisms." *FEMS Microbiology Reviews* 37, no. 5 (2013): 634–63.

140 **It's been shown that:** Delory, Benjamin M., Pierre Delaplace, Marie-Laure Fauconnier, and Patrick Du Jardin. "Root-emitted volatile organic compounds: can they mediate belowground plant-plant interactions?" *Plant and Soil* 402, nos. 1–2 (2016): 1–26.

INDEX

fitness routines, 20
flower gardens, 12–13
Flower Mission of New York initiative, 42
flow of garden, 151
food, 77–78
foraging, 127
forest bath *(Shinrin-yoku)*, 39–40
forests, 11–12
forsythias *(Forsythia x intermedia)*,
    12–13
Forsythia x intermedia, 12–13
fracking, 67–68, 78
Fraissinet, Peter, 97, 99–100
Frazer, Tammy, 160–61
Fraxinus sp., 68–69
fuchsia *(Cordyline* sp.), 27
fungal mycorrhizae, 131, 135, 140
fungi, 140
furyū monji, 84

Gandhi, Mahatma, 147
Gardens by the Bay, 29
gardens / gardening
    community, 59–60, 163–64
    conditions in, 13
    flower, 12–13
    flow of, 151
    houseplants *(See* houseplants)
    Millennials and, 20
    regular care and, 14
    vegetable, 13
Gaultheria procumbens, 11–12
geosmin, 161–62
going on a plant date exercise, 122–23
gooseberry *(Ribes hirtellum)*, 13
Graf, Alfred Byrd, 104–5
Grassy Island Creek, restoration of, 65–66,
    68–69
gray birch *(Betula populifolia)*, 65
Great Bear Rainforest, 71–74
Greek empire, 96
green color of plants, reason for, 129–30
greenhouses
    in early 1900s, 104–5
    first wooden, 96
    Roman *specularium*, 96

habits
    caregiving habits and mind-set,
        developing, 111–12
    identity-based, 91–92
    outcome-based, 91–92
Hamamelis virginiana, 160
Hanging Gardens of Babylon, 95–96
Hayes, Randy, 85
healing powers of plants, 15, 32–34
    community change and, 40–42
    horticultural therapy *(See* horticultural
        therapy)
    therapeutic horticulture, 43–45
Hedera helix, 159
Hemerocallis sp., 12–13
hemlock *(Tsuga* sp.), 131
herbarium collections, 97–101
herbs, 130, 144
hollyhocks *(Alcea* sp.), 12–13
horticultural therapy, 35–40
    autism and, 35–37
    cardiopulmonary rehabilitation and, 36
    dementia and, 36–37
    historical uses of, 39
    in hospital setting, 36
    Shinrin-yoku (forest bath), 39–40
    stress and, 37–39
houseplants, 14, 40, 89–107
    Amazonian cultures, crops cultivated
        by, 94
    building routine as gardener, 91–92
    Chinese gardens, 95
    discovery exercise, 106–7
    environment for plants to thrive, creating
        (See environment in which plants
        thrive)
    first greenhouses, 96
    in Greek empire, 96
    greenhouses and nurseries, early 1900s,
        104–5
    herbarium collections, cataloged and
        preserved in, 97–101
    as human construct, 94
    Japanese gardens, 95
    knowing your plants *(See* knowing
        plants)